Yes, You Are Being Judged: A Realist's Guide to Job Searching

For permission requests, write to the publisher at:
Purple Acorn Press (an imprint of Gently Ventures, Inc.)
Silver Spring, MD | https://www.gentlyventures.com

Book and Cover design by Gently Ventures, Inc.

ISBN: 979-8-9994468-0-0

Printed in the United States of America
First Edition

Yes, You Are Being Judged: A Realist's Guide to Job Searching

Mike Peditto

Dedication

To Karen, Carson, and Isabella, may you always think I'm cool for writing a book.

To Pat Peditto for liking every single LinkedIn and Instagram post I make.

And to Dr. John Peditto, who would have loved trying to explain to his friends that his son is an internet influencer.

Contents

Introduction: A Skill, Not a Crisis

Welcome to the Mess

Nobody plans to read a job search book until they absolutely have to. If you're reading this, there's a good chance something pushed you here. Maybe it was a layoff. Maybe it was the slow burn of a job that used to be tolerable but now feels like it's eating your soul one Slack message at a time. Or maybe it's that creeping feeling that you've outgrown your current gig, even if nothing is technically wrong. Whatever brought you here, welcome. And I mean that sincerely because it takes a weird kind of courage to admit you're not where you want to be.

Now, let's be honest: Job searching is a mess. It's not a process as much as it's a psychological experiment being conducted on you without your consent. You spend hours tweaking your resume, customizing cover letters that may or may not be read, clicking "apply now" for jobs that ghost you harder than your high school prom date, and just hoping that somehow a recruiter picks your resume off a giant pile and wants to talk to you. And when they do? They want to schedule a call to talk about a job that pays 40% less than your current salary, requires eight years of experience in a niche platform invented three years ago, and offers pizza parties as a benefit.

It's no wonder you can't log in to social media without seeing 100 new videos of somebody stuck in a nightmare job search. And the worst part is, no one ever taught us how to do this. Seriously. You spend years learning that mitochondria are the powerhouse of the cell and that World War I started with the assassination of Archduke Franz Ferdinand, but nobody pulls you aside in high school and says, "Hey, just so you know, your ability to craft a resume, communicate your value, and navigate systems built to confuse you will determine half your professional life." Cool cool cool. The fact that I didn't even have to look those things up and still remember them all these years after graduation says it all!

So we stumble through it. We google interview tips. We sign up for newsletters that promise the "Five Secrets to Stand Out in Your Job Search." We watch TikTok videos by people who don't seem old enough to have ever had a job and seem only to be repeating what they googled. We feel bad for not knowing how this works, as if it's a personal failure instead of what it actually is: a big, big, big, big (how many times can I write big before you stop reading?), big ol' mess!

And that brings us to why this book exists. Not because I think you need a motivational speech. You don't need inspiration. You need real talk. You need a system that works in *this* market, with *your* experience, for your goals. This is not some generic book about "acing the interview," like some robot from a career center handout. It's about understanding how interviews actually work, why hiring is a hot mess, why good people get rejected for dumb reasons, and how to stop being surprised by it. I'm not here to give you scripts to memorize that only work in a vacuum or tell you that if you manifest hard enough, the right job will find you. I'm here to show you how to run a job search like someone who knows what they're doing. Whether you're reading this in full-blown panic mode or you're just kind of job-curious and wondering if there's something better out there, you're in the right place.

Here's the shift I want you to make right now, before you even turn the page: Job searching is not a crisis. It's not a punishment. It's not the professional equivalent of being benched. It's a skill. And like any other skill, you can get better at it. You can learn how to write a resume that works, navigate interviews without blacking out, ask better questions, and negotiate like someone who doesn't panic when numbers come up. These are not magic traits reserved for the lucky and the charismatic. These are skills you can learn, the kind that, once you learn them, will be yours forever.

Because let's say the unsaid here: You will do this again. This isn't your last job search. Even if you land the perfect role after reading this, at some point, you'll be back on the market. That's not failure. That's reality. Careers are long, winding, weird things, and the people who do the best are the ones who get good at navigating transitions, not just coasting when things are fine.

I will not pretend the process is fair. I will not sell you on a dream in which effort always equals outcome. I always tell people, I'm not your career bestie here to make you feel invincible. If you want pep talks and hand-holding, I'm not your guy. But I can help you show up like a professional who understands the game and how to be good at it. I'll be real. It'll be strategic. I'll probably make you laugh at least a few times, and even if I don't, please tell me I did anyway. And by the end of this book, you won't just stop worrying about being steamrolled by the judgment of a job search, you'll know how to shape it yourself.

Welcome to the mess. Yes, you are being judged. Let's make that work for you.

Who the Hell Is Mike Peditto? Why Should I Care What He Has To Say?

This is the part where I'm supposed to rattle off a bunch of impressive things about myself so you'll believe that I know what I'm talking about. But if we're being honest—and this book will be brutally honest—I'm not here because I've had a perfect career. I'm here because I've had the opposite.

I've been laid off. I've been fired. I've searched for a job in front of millions of viewers online. I've had interviews I bombed so hard that I still cringe about them in the shower years later. I've applied to jobs I knew I was a perfect fit for and still been ghosted. I've ignored my own advice because I was spiraling. I've had the maybe-if-I-just-apply-to-more-jobs panic-apply session at 1 a.m. I've made every mistake I talk about in this book. And I'm going to share a lot of my own real, embarrassing stories with you as we go.

That's where this all started. Not from some polished career path but out of frustration, from being fed up with how complicated, secretive, and frankly stupid the job search process felt. Then I did something that a lot of people considered professionally reckless: I started talking about it. Publicly. On TikTok.

I started posting videos about what it was like to search for a job after being laid off, what I was doing, what was working, what was not working, and what made me want to scream into the void. I was honest, maybe even a little too honest. And the weird thing is, people didn't run away. They leaned in. Because it turns out, everyone hates this process. And no one with my experience on the hiring side was talking about it in a way that felt real. So I kept posting.

And then something I truly never expected happened. The videos started going viral, over and over again. Not because they were polished or professionally lit (they definitely were not), but because they hit a nerve. People were showing up by the thousands to my daily job searching live streams and watching me strike a balance between trying to figure out my own career while giving actual good and experienced advice at the same time. It wasn't just because I was the expert. It was because I was doing what no other "job search gurus" were doing, being honest and vulnerable. It was about giving people a look behind the curtain at how hiring *actually* works.

That was the beginning of Realistic Recruiting. I wasn't just a guy yelling about resumes into his phone or a 24-year-old who had just landed their first job and was now selling career advice. I'd already spent years in recruiting, talent acquisition, and hiring strategy. I'd read thousands of resumes, interviewed thousands of candidates, and sat in those behind-closed-doors hiring debriefs where really good candidates were rejected for really dumb reasons. I've been the guy advocating for a candidate and arguing with hiring managers for passing on them for not sending a thank-you note. I've watched candidates be passed over because someone on the hiring side didn't like their energy, which I then needed to figure out how to communicate to the candidate. I've dealt with hiring managers who wanted to "go in a different direction," which is usually corporate-speak for "We don't know why. We just aren't going to hire this person." That's the stuff most "gurus" don't tell you about because they aren't actually in the room where it happens. But I am in the room, so I started telling people about it.

As I spoke to more and more job seekers, the gap between the help and advice they needed and what they were getting from everyone else only became more evident, so I started filling in that gap, one video at a time. I became that guy who makes career content that doesn't sound like the career content you hear from everyone else. I'm not a guru. I'm not a coach selling you a $1500 course. Just a real person who's been on both sides of the hiring table, who knows the rules, knows when to break them, and knows how to explain it all in a way that doesn't make you want to slam your laptop shut.

And when I went back to a full-time job, I kept Realistic Recruiting going. I wasn't some former recruiter selling secrets; I was somebody still working in the industry, doing my best not to be the kind of human resources person you hate. I've built hiring processes from scratch. I've coached teams on how to actually assess candidates beyond their gut feeling. I've helped shape what good hiring should look like. And still, every day, I talk to people who feel completely lost because they applied to 200 jobs and haven't gotten one response. Or they finally had an interview, crushed it, then never heard back. Or they negotiated an offer, and the company pulled it. Or they're wondering if they're too old, too junior, too weird, too… something. The answer is no. You're not too anything. You're just stuck in a system that is hard to navigate.

I don't pretend to have all the answers. But I do have a hell of a lot of experience, on the inside and the outside. I've been the candidate, the recruiter, the hiring manager, the team builder, the public job hunter, the TikTok guy, the corporate guy, the Linked-Influencer, the burnout guy, and now… the guy who wrote this book.

If you're looking for someone with a perfect LinkedIn feed, that's not me. But if you want someone who will tell you the truth, explain the system, and help you navigate it strategically while maintaining your sanity, then you've come to the right place.

That's who I am. That's why I'm here. And if you're still reading, that probably means you're ready to do this differently. Let's go.

This Is a Skill, Not a Crisis

Let's get something straight up front: Job searching shouldn't be something you only do in an emergency. It's not something you only dust off when you've been laid off, ghosted by your boss, or hit the career equivalent of rock bottom. It feels like a crisis—because that's when most of us engage with it—but it isn't one. It's a skill. A real, teachable, repeatable skill that no one ever taught you, but you're expected to be great at anyway.

Think about it: If you were terrible at negotiating a lease or writing a business plan, you wouldn't assume you were just a flawed human. You'd (hopefully) say, "Huh, maybe I should learn how to do that." But job searching? When that doesn't go well, most people internalize it as a character flaw, like they're not charismatic enough, too unattractive, too much or not enough of something, because they didn't get called back. Because they got ghosted. Because they keep getting to the final round and then hearing, "We decided to move in a different direction." It's not you. It's the fact that job searching, like any other professional skill, has its own rules and expectations, and you need to understand them.

Let's talk about what job searching actually means. It's not just writing a better resume or figuring out what the hell a professional brand is. It's knowing how to:

- Communicate your value to people who have zero context and short attention spans.
- Understand what hiring managers are actually looking for in a candidate. Spoiler: it's rarely just what's written in the job description.
- Navigate rejection without spiraling.
- Interpret recruiter behavior that often makes no sense.
- Negotiate without breaking out in stress hives.
- Build visibility before you need it.
- Talk about what you do in a way that makes people want to work with you.

These are all skills. And the beautiful thing about skills? You can cultivate them through practice, feedback, and iteration, just like any other part of your professional life.

I made all the mistakes before I started reviewing resumes and hiring people myself. All of them. I took a spray-and-pray approach and applied to any job I could find. I had a resume with a 3D WordArt header. (Yes, really. I don't want to talk about it.) I interviewed as if there was no way to prepare or be good at it. I said things like "I'm a people person" with a straight face. And I just assumed that I wasn't getting the offer because the manager was an idiot.

Fast forward to now, and here's what's different: I don't panic. I don't guess. I don't just hope for the best. I know how to target roles that make sense for me. I know how to talk about my work. I know how to run a search. And I've helped thousands of people do the same. I literally got a company to create a job for me because I knew how to present myself as someone they needed. That may not be the most common case, but it is still a realistic option. You're not just looking for a job this time. You're looking for jobs over time. The average person changes roles more than a dozen times in their career. That means learning how to job search is one of the most important long-term professional skills you can develop. It's not something to survive once and then forget. It's something to get really good at.

Think about the freedom that comes with knowing you could land something new, not only when your hand is forced, not if your company goes under, but anytime you decide you're ready. That's the difference between feeling trapped in your career and feeling in control of it. That's what this book is going to help you create.

So if you've been treating your job search like a fire you're constantly putting out, forget the hose. Let's build you a freaking fire escape. Let's build the tools you need so the next time something shifts, which it will, you're not reacting in crisis mode. You'll be ready with a strategy.

What This Book Actually Gives You

Let's be honest about what you probably expected when you picked up this book. Some mix of motivational fluff and bland, copy-paste job advice you could find in a LinkedIn carousel post, maybe a checklist, a template or two, and a few well-intentioned-but-useless affirmations like "Believe in yourself!" or "Your dream job is out there!" And hey, I get it. That's what a lot of career books do. They give you hope but not much help. So let me be clear: this book is not that.

You will not find one-size-fits-all scripts that guarantee a job offer if you just send them to enough strangers. You won't find a five-step plan to hack the algorithm and beat the ATS forever. There's no magic font size that unlocks recruiter attention. This isn't a workbook full of homework I expect you to complete like it's a group therapy retreat. And I'm definitely not going to tell you that if you just "manifest the right energy," the job will come.

What you will find is a real strategy. Real talk. Real frameworks. Things that work when the job market is hot *and* when it's trash. You'll find the stuff I've tested over and over again on myself, on job seekers I've coached, on hiring teams I've led, and the stuff that works for *real people* with *real lives* who don't have time to write thousand-word cover letters for a job that might not even exist next week.

You'll learn how to write a resume that doesn't just say you're "results-oriented" but really shows it. You'll get clarity on what makes a good LinkedIn profile actually good. Hint: it's not about whether you use the open-to-work banner! You'll finally understand what makes outreach work, not because you're bothering people into hiring you, but because you're reaching out with clarity, intention, and value. You'll stop walking into interviews hoping to "vibe well" and start walking in ready to communicate why you're a yes and not a maybe.

And because the job search isn't just tactical—it's emotional—you'll also learn how to deal with the parts that no one prepares you for: the ghosting, the rejection, the waiting, the energy dips, the motivation spirals, and the what-am-I-even-doing-with-my-life moments that hit after the third unanswered application in a row. This book doesn't just teach you how to do the thing. It helps you survive the part that feels like the thing isn't working.

I will not tell you that if you follow everything in here perfectly, you'll land your dream job. Anyone who promises that is lying to you. But I *will* tell you that this book will make you better and smarter at navigating every part of the job search more strategically, better prepared, and with more confidence, even if your confidence is MIA right now.

What you won't get from this book is false hope. You *will* get:

- A toolkit that works whether you're unemployed, underpaid, or just quietly plotting your next move.
- A no-fluff guide to resumes, outreach, interviewing, negotiation, and follow-up that cuts out the noise.
- The perspective of someone who's been on *both* sides of the hiring table in the current job market, not somebody telling you what we used to do back in 2009.
- A bunch of slightly-too-honest stories that will probably make you laugh and also make you feel very seen.
- A strategy you can actually apply, not just a philosophy to admire.

You also have permission to skip around and use this book like a buffet, not a prescription. If you're not networking right now, skip that chapter. If you're already in the offer stage, go straight to negotiation. Hit the epilogue if you just want to feel less alone after your latest rejection. There's no gold star for reading this thing front to back like a textbook. The win here is applying what makes sense, when it makes sense, for where you are.

So no, I'm not going to promise that this book will change your life. But I am going to promise it gives you the tools to change your approach and that, when you do, everything else gets easier. Because job searching isn't just about landing the job, it's about learning how to *search like someone who already knows their value.* That's what this book will give you. And that's why it works.

CHAPTER ONE

Your Job Search Phase

TL;DR

Most people see job searching as binary—you're either frantically applying to anything or comfortably employed. The reality? It's a spectrum, and your position on it determines what strategies will actually work.

When you use the wrong approach, you waste time and energy. Some people blast out applications for jobs they don't want. Others passively browse, missing opportunities that slip by. Many explore options without direction, stuck in career limbo.

Job searching is a skill, one that changes depending on your circumstances. Whether you're casually browsing, actively exploring, selectively applying, or urgently searching, each phase requires a different playbook.

This chapter will help you identify exactly where you are, apply the right strategy for your situation, and avoid common traps that frustrate most job seekers. You'll learn to replace panic with process, position yourself as the candidate companies chase, and take control of your career trajectory.

No more throwing resumes into the void. It's time to get strategic.

The Job Search Spectrum: Where Are You?

If you're reading this book, you have undoubtedly been frustrated that there is too much job search advice and that it is all kinds of contradictory. You're right, there is, and it is! There are some things you'll hear me say all the time that a lot of other *"experts"* don't agree with. I say *maybe* a lot. *Maybe* that will work. *Maybe* it won't. There is so much advice because different strategies can work in different situations. There is no single perfect way or answer. Job searching is ultimately a failure activity—meaning, most of the time, you aren't going to get the job. But that doesn't mean you did it wrong or followed bad advice. Every job seeker, every recruiter, and every manager is a unique human, and there is no universal answer to the question of what they are looking for. We can't control what will or won't work in any situation or what one manager will do versus another manager, but we can control how we strategize, prepare, and approach our job search. Job searching isn't a simple binary activity—it exists on a spectrum, and knowing where you are on that spectrum can help you strategize and waste less time and emotional energy trying to land a job.

Some people wait until they urgently need a job and then fire off 50 applications a day and wonder why they don't hear anything back. You'll hear people say how they've applied to a thousand jobs and can't get an interview, almost as if it's a badge of honor to apply to as many jobs as possible. Meanwhile, I promise you they were not qualified for a thousand jobs. Others browse passively, assuming someone is coming to save them with their dream job if they just want it enough. And then there are the explorers, people who know they want a change but aren't sure what their next step should be. These people end up in career limbo.

Here's the truth: Job searching is a skill. If you learn the skill and apply the right strategy for where you are, you'll get better results with less stress. But if you treat it like a last-minute scramble—or worse, do nothing and hope for the best—you'll always feel out of control.

Why Identifying Your Phase Matters

Each stage of the job search demands a different strategy. Blasting out 100 applications is a complete waste of time if you're in passive browsing mode. It's a waste of time in every phase, to be honest. On the flip side, if you're in an urgent job-search phase, casually liking LinkedIn posts and waiting for recruiters to notice you isn't going to cut it either.

Using the wrong strategy for your phase will lead to frustration and burnout. Applying blindly is exhausting and inefficient. The more time you spend on low-return activities, the more likely you are to feel stuck. But when you focus on high-impact actions—networking, referrals, and tailored applications—you'll see results faster and with way less stress.

If you don't know where you are in your job search, you're probably using the wrong strategy. Instead of guessing—or worse, panicking—identify your phase, adjust your approach, and start making moves that actually work. No more throwing resumes into the void. Be intentional. Here are some tips on how to shift from phase to phase:

From passive to exploratory: Start engaging on LinkedIn, update your resume, and track companies you admire.
From exploratory to active search: Begin reaching out to connections and customizing applications.
From active to urgent: Put out a call to action for your connections, prioritize high-impact applications, and reach out directly to hiring managers.

Understanding where you are in the job search spectrum also helps set realistic expectations. If you're just starting to explore, don't expect job offers to roll in overnight. But if you lay the groundwork early to position yourself as a strong candidate people want to hire, you'll be ahead of the game when the right role opens up.

The Four Phases of the Job Search Spectrum

Phase	What It Means	Best Strategies	Biggest Mistakes
Passive Browsing	You're happy in your job but open to better opportunities.	• Keep LinkedIn optimized • Casually network • Stay visible in industry conversations and events • Share insights	• Ignoring your network until you need a job • Not engaging on LinkedIn
Exploratory Mode	You're considering a change but not yet actively applying.	• Researching companies before you need a job • Update your resume • Start networking strategically	• Jumping into applications before you know what you want • Sending out generic applications too early makes you look unfocused
Active Search (Still Employed)	You're selectively applying while working.	• Casually reach out to people you know • Consider finding a third-party recruiter you trust. • Optimize LinkedIn for job seeker mode • Limit your applications	• Applying randomly • Not taking advantage of LinkedIn for the SEO factors (more on this later)
Urgent Job Search	You need a job ASAP.	• Ask for help • Reach out directly to hiring managers and recruiters • Focus on quality, well-researched, polished applications over quantity	• Mass-applying • Being too proud to get help • Panic applying to 983 roles

A Real World Success Story

Laura had been working as a recruiter for a tech giant for several years. She liked the work, but something felt off. Leadership's messages started to change, and she could feel the market starting to shift. She wasn't ready to apply yet, but she could read the writing on the wall and wanted to be ready for when the time came. She was in exploratory mode.

Instead of blindly applying to roles that she wasn't even sure she would want, Laura took a strategic approach. She researched companies that aligned with her goals. She started engaging with hiring managers and employees at those companies on LinkedIn, not by asking for a job but by commenting on their work and sharing insights. She also attended industry webinars and virtual networking events, where she introduced herself to decision-makers.

After a few months, it turned out that Laura's instincts were right, and the layoff notice came. While, of course, she felt some panic, the first thing she did was reach out to the connections she had built over the last few months at the companies that she was interested in and where she had cultivated connections. Based on previous interactions and their familiarity with Laura, one of them went to a higher-up in the company and fought to create a new role for her on their team. They already saw Laura as a strong fit, and she was the only person in line for a role that didn't exist until just then.

Mike's take: If you're considering a career move, start networking and researching early. A story like this may not always be how this goes, but when you hear people talk about networking, this is what they mean. By the time you need a job, it is probably too late just to be lacing up your shoes.

How to Avoid the Spray-and-Pray Trap

Most job seekers will experience it at some point: full-blown spray-and-pray mode. Maybe you just got laid off. Maybe you're miserable at your job. Maybe you've been applying for months with zero traction, and now you're willing to take *anything* that comes your way. Whatever the trigger, you find yourself frantically firing off applications to every vaguely relevant job posting with the hope that *something* will stick. But here's the problem: panic applying doesn't work.

I've been there. On my own job search tracking sheets, I can see all the moments I took the spray-and-pray approach. In the moment, it felt like I was getting somewhere, but the result was always long gaps without interviews and just racking up numbers of applications like it was some kind of badge of honor. Let me tell you: As someone who also sits on the hiring side, I can tell when people are panic applying for everything they see. And while I understand why they are doing it, it doesn't get them the job. People don't believe me when I say this—and I have the comment section battle scars to prove it—but the majority of applicants to most jobs are not even close to qualified. They may think they can do the job, but that is not the same as meeting the qualifications of the job. I'm not talking about a close-but-no-cigar fit. I'm talking about applications that just don't make sense. The shoot-your-shot mentality is great in a strong job market, but today, it's usually a waste of your time and energy. If you've sent out 100+ applications and gotten nowhere, it's not just bad luck. It's a bad strategy too.

Instead of mass-applying, work smarter. Keep your job search focused and high-impact. Here's how:

Apply to fewer well-researched, high-quality jobs per week. Prioritize roles that actually align with your skills and goals, where you can point to the requirements and show exactly where your resume demonstrates that you're qualified.

Research the company before applying. Do you actually want to work there? Are they growing or downsizing?

Look for opportunities where you can make an impact.

Hiring managers don't want someone who just wants a job. They want someone who will make them look good.

Use warm introductions whenever possible. I know you hear this a lot. Don't worry. We'll talk about long-term networking later.

Share consistently on LinkedIn and engage with others. Who cares if nobody likes it at first? Stop worrying about being cringe and start worrying about what gets people hired.

Refine your job search assets every week. Build a resume, LinkedIn profile, or portfolio related to your field. Treat your search like a project, not a slot machine.

Mix applications, networking, and personal branding. The best candidates don't *just* apply. They build relationships and make themselves visible.

As counterintuitive as it may feel, you'll get better results and minimize job search fatigue by focusing on quality over quantity. Here's the step-by-step strategy:

1. **Pause.** Before you hit "apply," ask, *Do I actually want this job, or am I just desperate*?
2. **Define your ideal job.** If you apply to everything, you end up with nothing. Get specific.
3. **Build a structured daily job search routine.** Include applications, networking, and skill-building.
4. **Track your progress.** Applying more isn't better. Applying better is better.

Panic applying doesn't get you hired. It gets you stuck. A focused, high-impact job search puts you in control, increases your chances of landing the right job, and keeps you sane along the way. Work smart, not desperate.

A Real World Success Story

I had recently made my first career move in six years and landed what I thought was a dream remote job. The job itself was okay, but it was not the job I expected, and it became clear to me that it was not going to be a long-term fit. I wasn't in danger of losing it, but it was also clear that staying there would stunt my career, so I decided to make a move when the right opportunity presented itself. I was still employed but in active search mode.

During this two-month search period, here is what I did. I made a list for myself of what I needed in a new job and what my greatest value would be out there in the great big corporate world. I tailored my resume and application for each job that fit all of my requirements. In fact, I only applied for ten jobs in those two months. If it didn't meet my requirements, I didn't waste my time. But if it did meet my requirements, I made sure they knew I was serious. I sent a LinkedIn message to the hiring manager for each role I applied to explaining that I had only been in my role for a short time, the reasons a move made sense for me now, and that I felt confident the role at their company would be a better long-term fit.

The strategy worked. I got interviews at eight of the ten roles I applied for, withdrew from processes when they didn't feel right, and continued to pursue the ones that really stood out. I wound up getting the ideal role for me, at the salary I said I required, and had the right opportunity to grow in exactly the right role for me at the time.

Mike's take: Not to pat myself on the back, but I love sharing my stories when I can. And I nailed this search. This is how job searching should work when you are searching while you're still getting a paycheck.

Laura (above) and I didn't just search blindly and throw a resume at anything we saw. We matched our strategies to our job-search phase, leveraged every strategy out there, and took a proactive approach. The result? Less wasted energy, more effective job searches without the frustration of mass-applying and getting nowhere. So, where are you in your job search? Are you using the right strategy?

Position Yourself as the Candidate Companies Chase

For some people, getting hired means applying for dozens of jobs, crossing their fingers, and hoping a recruiter picks them out of a sea of similar applicants. But that's only one way to get a job. The best candidates don't just apply—they make companies come to them.

Your LinkedIn profile (which we'll talk about more in chapter three) isn't just a digital resume—it's a searchable portfolio that recruiters actively scan for potential candidates. If they can't find you, they can't hire you. That's why optimizing your profile is non-negotiable. Your headline should go beyond just a job title. Something like "Marketing Manager" is forgettable, but "Data-Driven Marketer | Driving Brand Growth & Engagement" immediately signals expertise. Your About section isn't a place for a lifeless bio. Instead, it should tell a compelling story about who you are, the problems you solve, and the value you bring to a team. In your Experience section, ditch generic job duties and instead highlight measurable results and impactful achievements. Recruiters search by skills, so make sure your top skills and endorsements align with your target roles to improve visibility. Finally, engagement is key. Commenting on industry posts, sharing insights, and interacting with leaders in your field increases your chances of being noticed. The more active you are, the more likely you'll be on a recruiter's radar when the right opportunity comes up.

Thought Leadership (Without Being a LinkedIn Influencer Wannabe)

I won't lie. I still cringe every day at the fact that I somehow became a LinkedIn influencer. While it has done wonderful things for my career, it was never who I planned to be. Like a lot of this stuff, it just kind of happened. You don't need to post daily, chase followers, or write essays to stand out on LinkedIn. You do need to accept, however, that some level of content engagement positions you as a credible professional, and a lot of people are getting great jobs because of their LinkedIn activity. Since I know you're already shaking your head and saying, "But how?" I'll get you started with a few ideas. (You're welcome!)

Commenting > Posting. Engaging with industry leaders is often more effective than posting your own content.
Share insights from your work. Lessons learned, quick case studies, or industry takeaways make you stand out.
Use LinkedIn articles for deeper insights. Writing one in-depth post about your field every month can boost your credibility.
Consistency matters more than frequency. One solid post every two weeks keeps you visible without being overwhelming.

Your LinkedIn profile matters. Recruiters look at it. Hiring managers look at it, and beyond that, using it well makes more people look at it. Every time you engage with a post on LinkedIn, the chances of someone new seeing your profile go up. Every time you post on LinkedIn—even if only one person interacts with it—every one of that person's connections can now see your post. You don't have to be an influencer, but *if you are only using LinkedIn as a job board, you are using it wrong!* These are the things that great job seekers realize. None of this is mandatory, but is your goal to get a job or just to make a point that you don't want to do it?

A Real World Success Story

Alexander didn't land his next job by blasting out 100 applications. He did it by showing up every single day for 100 days. Instead of chasing recruiters, he made them come to him. What was his strategy? He wrote about his field every day on LinkedIn. He posted insights on software engineering, career lessons, and problem-solving approaches. He shared personal reflections, breaking down what worked, what didn't, and how he was improving at his craft. He engaged with his industry, replied to comments, joined discussions, and built relationships with professionals he respected.

At first, nothing happened. Then, his posts started gaining traction. People recognized his name. His network expanded. Hiring managers started following his content. And while he doesn't explicitly say this landed him a job, one thing is clear: He's no longer another engineer scrolling job boards. He's a professional people come to when they have opportunities.

> **Mike's Take:** Want to stand out? Be visible. Build a personal brand before you need a job. Or don't because you don't want to, but now you know that others are doing it and that if you don't, you're making the choice to let them be first in line for the job.

Why a Portfolio, Website, or Public Work Can Set You Apart

A portfolio is non-negotiable if you are looking for a new role in a creative or technical field. But even in non-creative industries, showcasing your expertise beyond a resume helps, especially if you are entry-level or trying to make a career pivot. Want to stand out over everybody else with the same experience (or lack of it)? Then show people your work! Pick the right elements to showcase, depending on your field. Here's what you can show off and why you should bother:

Portfolios for design, writing, or development roles. If your work is visible and verifiable, you gain instant credibility.
Case studies or a personal blog for business roles. Sharing problem-solving approaches and successful projects proves your expertise.
Public speaking, panels, or webinars. If you've spoken at events or shared insights in your industry, highlight that on your LinkedIn.
Side projects or open-source work. Especially for engineers, showing real-world contributions speaks louder than a resume.

SIDEBAR

Right now, you're probably saying, "But I shouldn't have to do all of this just to get a job." Here's another one of those things I'll say that a lot of other people won't: You're right. You shouldn't! But, in life, there is often a big difference between how we want it to be and how it is, and this is one of those times. You may have seen me doing magic tricks on TikTok, but I'm not actually a magician. I can't wave my wand and make it easier to get a job. I'm also cheering for everything to get easier and would love a world where nobody has to put this much effort in just to pay the bills, but it is what it is. So let's focus on what helps people get the job. Here is another success story for inspiration and motivation.

A Real World Success Story

Sarah didn't find her next job by spamming applications. She found it by being in the right room at the right time. Instead of competing with hundreds of applicants on job boards, she embedded herself in a niche Slack community where hiring managers, industry experts, and data professionals connected. She joined Locally Optimistic, a private Slack group for analytics professionals, where data leaders discuss trends, challenges, and, occasionally, job openings. She introduced herself and shared about her career transition from education to data analytics and her interest in breaking into the field. She engaged with the community, responded to discussions, asked smart questions, and contributed positively where she could.

Within days, a hiring manager from edX, a top online education company, sent her a DM. There was no job posting or public hiring announcement. They had a need, saw her engagement, and reached out before the role even hit the job boards. One conversation turned into an interview, which turned into a job offer for a content data analyst role.

Mike's take: Private industry groups (Slack, Discord, niche forums) are gold mines not only for job opportunities but for real networking (again, we will discuss this lots later). I am in several Slack groups, one just for dads looking for a place to talk with other dads. Nobody has ever joined the group saying, "Somebody hire me. I'm networking," but I have 100% seen real connections and job opportunities come to people as a result of the time they spent in this group.

Most job seekers grind through applications, hoping for a response. The most successful ones? They make hiring managers come to them. Alexander didn't beg for interviews—he became so visible that recruiters couldn't ignore him. Sarah didn't let herself get lost in a pile of resumes. She was already in the right place when the opportunity arose.

The best jobs aren't always posted. They go to the people already in the conversation, the ones sharing their insights, engaging with the right communities, and showing up where decision-makers are paying attention. Want to stop competing with 300 applicants? Stop relying on the lowest effort job searching approach that everybody else is doing, and start being impossible to ignore. Build relationships, share what you know, and be active in the spaces where opportunities appear. I reiterate: How we want it to be and how it is are not the same thing!

The Emotional Impact of Job Searching

It's important to acknowledge that job searching can be an emotional rollercoaster. The highs of landing an interview can quickly be followed by the lows of ghosting or rejection. Understanding that this process is not a reflection of your worth is key. As a society, we have been programmed to tie our worth to our job. Hell, most of us can't even get our teeth looked at if we don't have a good job. I wish I knew how to make this better, but I don't. I went through so many daily battles with myself during my own job search. I gained weight. I stopped engaging in the hobbies that made me happy. And I carried an unfair burden on my shoulders... You know, human stuff. I don't know the magic words to make you not feel this way, but I do want you to know that if you do feel this way, I see you, and I get it, and so do many others.

I get asked a lot about how to stay motivated, and the truth is that it's okay not to always be motivated. Motivation is not a straight line. It's a roller coaster that goes up and down. Some days, you'll feel great, and other days, you'll feel like life kicked you in the stomach, and all you want to do is lie on the floor. They are both okay to feel for that day. Many successful professionals face long periods of job-search struggles, but only you have the power to make sure that you have a structured daily routine, track your progress, and take mental breaks to prevent burnout. Job searching is as much about resilience as it is about tactics.

I've been there. I've applied, out of fear, to jobs I didn't really want. I've sent out dozens of applications and heard nothing back. And I've also seen the power of networking, the impact of a strategic application, and how positioning yourself the right way makes all the difference.

Your job search shouldn't feel like a chaotic, never-ending loop. Once you recognize where you are in the process and apply the right strategies, you'll start to feel in control again. That's when the real opportunities start rolling in.

Mike's Snarky Do's and Don'ts of Job Searching

DO identify where you are on the job search spectrum. I gave you a chart. Just go figure it out.

DO tailor your approach to your phase. Basically, you should always be doing some kind of job search activity!

DO take your time on applications. Ten well-researched, tailored applications are better than 50 generic ones, unless your goal is going viral on TikTok by talking about all your applications.

DO optimize your LinkedIn. Recruiters are searching for candidates every day. LinkedIn is a giant professional search engine, and you have to focus on SEO.

DON'T apply to everything in sight. Quantity doesn't equal quality. Please stop making me look at marketing associate resumes when I'm hiring a C.M.O.

DON'T wait until you're unemployed to start networking. It's already too late for this search, but do it anyway for the next one.

DON'T ignore your online presence. I'd rather be cringe than unemployed. But hey, that's just me.

DON'T just sit back and wait. If you're not actively positioning yourself as someone companies want to hire, you'll always be chasing opportunities instead of attracting them.

Spray-and-pray doesn't get you hired. It gets you stuck. A focused, high-impact job search puts you in control, increases your chances of landing the right job, and keeps you sane along the way.

The best job seekers don't just apply for jobs—they position themselves for opportunities. When you optimize your online presence, build relationships, and tailor your approach based on where you are in your career, you stop begging for jobs and start choosing them.

CHAPTER TWO

The Foundations of a Standout Resume

TL;DR

Your resume isn't a historical record—it's a strategic marketing tool designed to pitch your value in seconds. When recruiters scan hundreds of applications, generic job descriptions and responsibility lists won't capture attention. The harsh reality? Hiring managers spend just six seconds deciding if your resume deserves closer review. In that brief window, it needs to communicate clearly why you are the solution to their problem.

This chapter breaks through the noise of outdated resume advice. You'll learn how Applicant Tracking Systems (ATS) actually work (hint: they're *not* designed to reject you), why the ARR method transforms bland job descriptions into compelling achievements, and how to create a document that stands out instead of blending in. No more wasted applications. No more wondering why you never hear back. It's time to craft a resume that opens doors instead of closing them.

Before We Begin

I have to say something before this chapter even starts. I hate talking about resumes and giving resume advice! Don't get me wrong. I can help you make your specific resume better. I've done it for countless people, but I hate giving resume advice. In fact, the only reason this chapter even exists is because my publisher told me I can't write a book about job searching and not include resume advice!

Why do I hate it? Because you can ask ten different people for resume advice and get ten different pieces of advice, and they are all correct. They are also all incorrect. There is no such thing as a perfect resume, and there is no such thing as perfect resume advice. The first TikTok video I ever made was me (much skinnier and with less grey hair) explaining that there are no universal answers to this stuff. If I tell you I don't care about a resume being two pages, and another recruiter says they won't read any resume longer than one page, we are both right.

Most resume "rules" are nothing more than someone's opinion being told to you as a fact. Resumes are such an important part of finding a job, but they are also the most frustrating part because of people's strong opinions.

So anytime you hear (or read, in this case) me giving resume advice, know that I generally speak from best practices and what I see work for people. If your resume breaks every one of my "rules" and gets you interviews, then ignore me. But if you are struggling, don't know where to turn, and trust that I am giving you the best advice I can—even as I admit that I'm just a guy with an opinion—you should read this chapter.

WTF is an ATS?

Let's come in hot right away and talk about the giant elephant in the room: Applicant tracking systems (ATS) are not out to get you. Despite what you've heard from some of my favorite TikTok and LinkedIn gurus who have never actually worked with an ATS, they're not some evil AI, rejecting candidates just for the fun of it. My job would be so much easier if I just had a mean robot that could reject all the bad applicants for me, but alas, it's just me and my tired, aging eyes reading each one. That said, these systems do have quirks, and if you don't understand how they work, you may be spending your time worrying about the wrong things.

Think of ATS software as a digital filing cabinet. Inside the ATS, I can create jobs, post them on our website, set up interview plans, schedule them, email candidates, and manage the entire hiring process. An ATS to a recruiter is no different than a CRM (customer relationship management) system like Hubspot is to a salesperson. What are the biggest ATS myths? That they automatically reject candidates who don't meet 100% of the job criteria, that PDFs are the enemy, or that if you don't have the perfect keyword match, you're doomed.

Some job applications do include what are known as knockout questions set by the hiring team such as, "Have you ever managed a team of 5+?" In this case, if that is a hard requirement for the role, the system may be programmed to reject everyone who answers no, but that is very different from robots deciding which resumes a recruiter will read.

Though most systems don't, some systems do have the ability to assign a resume a score based on how often keywords show up, but every recruiter knows those scores are not very reliable and that they still need to look at the resumes. But also, if your resume is getting a really bad score in these systems, that is probably not the system's fault, and most people are just too scared to tell you that. We will talk a bit more about how to get a higher score in those situations. Still, the reality is that people who are really, genuinely qualified for the job are either getting higher scores already, as they should, or they just have a really terrible resume.

ATS Myths That Are Wasting Your Time

ATS rejects resumes that aren't an exact match. False. But it can rank candidates based on the content of their resumes. You don't need every keyword, but you do need the ones that actually describe the job. Not taking the time to edit your resume and reflect the sought-after experience and skill set is willful incompetence, to be honest.

A human never sees my resume. Wrong. Outside of knockout questions, the only way a resume can be rejected is through human review. I can't promise you that every recruiter reads every resume, but human recruiters hit the *reject* button.

Using a Word Doc automatically disqualifies you. Nope. Most modern ATS software can read PDFs, Word files, or .txt files just fine. In fact, ATS systems really don't struggle that much with columns or formatting the way some would have you believe. Almost every resume I see shows up just fine in the ATS, no matter how over-designed.

Fancy design makes me stand out. Nope, not in a good way. Outside of design-related roles, it's best to stick to clean, simple formatting, not because of the ATS, but because you want your resume to be about what's written in it!

Now that you know the truth, you can stop fearing this imaginary enemy.

SIDEBAR

Have you ever heard of the white font trick? For as long as the ATS has existed, people have been giving the same dumb advice and going viral for it. In this case, you will hear people tell you that they copied the job description and pasted it into their resume, made it 1 pt size and changed the font to white so it doesn't show up to the human eye and then they can pass through the ATS.

Let me be clear that this has never worked and will never work. Even in a world where what you've heard about the ATS is true—and it isn't—and you now receive a 100% score, the next step in the process will be the recruiter seeing your 100% score, opening your resume and having no clue how you got a 100% score because it is missing all of the information they need to see. Free will is real. They don't need to interview you just because you got a 100%. Not to mention, if all of the stuff they need to see is on your resume because it's true, then you didn't even need to do this. Just don't. I promise it doesn't work, and I promise every recruiter will know exactly what happened.

The ATS isn't your enemy—it's just a tool recruiters use to manage applications. Your goal isn't to "trick" it. The truth is that there are a lot of people who are not experienced enough to talk about the ATS who use fear tactics to sell you products or coaching. I've called them out time and time again, but like the tech bro who just hustles harder, these stories just won't go away.

Okay, that's enough ATS talk. Time to focus on making your resume stand out to humans because they're the ones who make the hiring decisions.

What Makes a Resume Sink or Swim

Within seconds of opening your resume, a hiring manager knows if it's worth reading or going straight to the no pile. The harsh truth? Most resumes fail this test. Not because the candidates aren't qualified but because their resumes are generic, forgettable, and painfully vague. Okay, they also go to the no pile because many candidates aren't really qualified. I'm going to keep saying this: Please stop applying for jobs you're not qualified for! Here's why generic resumes fail:

They make the recruiter do the work. If your resume forces recruiters to dig for relevant information, they won't. They may have *hundreds* of resumes to scan. If yours doesn't immediately communicate value, it won't get read. (Yes, I know that as you read that, your hatred of recruiters grew.)

They sound like everyone else. "Results-driven professional with excellent communication skills" means nothing. Your resume should distinguish you, set you apart, not drown you in buzzwords.

They're a list of responsibilities when you need impact. Hiring managers don't care what work you were assigned or what tasks you were given. They care about what you accomplish and what value you bring.

One of the biggest mistakes job seekers make is listing responsibilities instead of impact. Recruiters don't care that you "managed a team" or "handled client accounts." They care about results. If your resume reads like a glorified job description, you're doing it wrong.

A strong resume doesn't just say what you did—it says why it mattered. Seeing is believing, and hiring managers need to see impact fast. We've talked about what makes a resume stand out, but now it's time to break it down visually. The difference between a bad resume and a great one isn't just what's on the page. It's how it's structured, worded, and formatted to communicate impact immediately. The time-to-value for a great resume is only a few seconds. This means that within a few seconds, I have to be able to find the two or three most valuable things I need to see to decide whether you're a potential fit for this job.

Feature	Bad Resume	Good Resume
Headline	"Experienced Marketing Professional"	"Growth-Focused Marketing Manager Who Drove 200% ROI in 2023"
Summary	"Hardworking and detail-oriented, seeking a role to utilize my skills"	"Digital marketing strategist with 7+ years of experience increasing conversion rates by 45% through data-driven campaigns"
Bullet Points	"Managed social media accounts"	"Increased LinkedIn engagement by 150% through targeted content strategy"
Metrics	None	Every bullet has a **measurable impact** (revenue growth, efficiency improvement, cost savings)
Formatting	Dense paragraphs, inconsistent fonts	Clean structure, easy to skim

A bad resume tells. A good resume shows. Your goal? Make it ridiculously easy for the recruiter or hiring manager to see your value fast. If I can't tell in the first third or half of a page why you are a fit for this job, I will probably never be able to tell.

Here's what you need to know:

Use standard formatting. I like a single-column layout with clear headings. Using multiple columns won't hurt you in the ATS, but it cuts down on the space you have to include what matters.

Optimize for keywords. Mirror the job description, but don't stuff your resume with meaningless fluff.

Use a readable font. Arial, Calibri, or Times New Roman at 10–12 pt size. Please stop making it hard to read your resume. My eyes get worse every year, and y'all keep cramming more and more tiny words onto the page!

Tailor every application. You *don't* need a brand-new resume each time, but you do need to adjust key skills and phrases based on the job description.

The A.R.R. Method

A resume isn't your life story. It's not a personal history lesson or a place to list every job you've ever had. It's a marketing tool—a sales pitch in written form—that should instantly communicate your value to hiring managers. If your resume isn't making it easy for someone to see why you're the right fit, it's failing.

Recruiters don't read resumes the way you think they do. They scan. They skim. And if your resume doesn't grab their attention, it's game over. You've probably heard that recruiters spend six to eight seconds reading your resume, and while that's not entirely true, it's also not entirely false. The truth is an experienced recruiter can usually tell in six to eight seconds if you are not even close—and as I've said, a lot of applicants are not even close. Your job in those six to eight seconds is to make it easy to see exactly what the recruiter needs to see so that they keep reading. If you have a good resume, the resume review won't be over after those six to eight seconds.

Most people's resumes are just a list of their responsibilities at their job. They look like what the manager will post online when looking for a replacement. Hiring managers don't care what you were assigned to do. They care about what you accomplished. Enter the ARR Method, which transforms bland, forgettable job descriptions into compelling, results-driven statements. Here's how it works:

Action: What did you do?

Resources: What tools, teams, or processes did you use?

Results: What was the measurable impact? Instead of "Managed a social media campaign," try "Led a social media campaign using paid ads and organic content, increased engagement by 40% in three months." See the difference? The second version proves impact instead of just listing a task.

Start with a strong action verb. Skip weak phrases like "responsible for" or "helped with." Use powerful verbs like *led, optimized,* and *transformed.*

Be specific about resources. Highlight tools, processes, or strategies you used. Did you implement new software? Lead a cross-functional team? Automate a workflow? Say so. Did you not have those resources? Say so because a lack of resources is still making use of resources.

End with a clear, measurable result. If you don't have hard numbers, use percentages, comparisons, or qualitative improvements. Instead of "Improved customer retention," say, "Increased customer retention by 25% through a targeted outreach program."

Before	After
Managed client accounts	Led a portfolio of 15 enterprise clients, increasing annual revenue by 20% through consultative sales strategies
Developed marketing materials	Created marketing collateral using Canva and HubSpot, contributing to a 35% increase in lead conversion
Handled onboarding for new hires	Streamlined new-hire onboarding process, reducing ramp-up time by 30% through an automated training module
Assisted with social media management	Developed and executed a content strategy that increased LinkedIn engagement by 50% in six months
Supported customer inquiries	Resolved 95% of customer tickets within SLA, leading to a 15% improvement in customer satisfaction scores
Assisted in recruitment efforts	Implemented a structured interview process that improved time-to-hire by 20% and raised candidate quality

But What if I Don't Have Numbers?

Ready for another one of those things that I say that nobody else will? Your resume doesn't need numbers in every bullet point. Yes, I do know there are numbers in all my examples. Numbers are great, and when you have them, you should use them. In some roles, like sales, including numbers is an absolute must.

A lot of you have more numbers than you realize. For example, as a profession, nurses tell me all the time that they don't have numbers to include on a resume. But every time a nurse tells me that in a coaching session, I start asking questions like, "Well, how many patients have you helped?" "What do the patient-care surveys say?" "How small was the staff?" It turns out not every number is a percentage increase.

But what if I *really* don't have the numbers? Okay, fine. Here is the part where I will say something nobody else will: Don't include numbers. Wild, right? But I want you to think about these two questions while you write your resume bullet points: 1. What did I do? 2. Why did it matter? Right now, you are probably saying, *But it didn't matter.* So let me rephrase. Why did it matter to the people it mattered to? You were being paid to do something to affect someone: to help a customer, to make someone money, to do something. What did you do, and why did it matter to them?

Here are the concrete ways to apply ARR to your resume right now:

Audit your bullet points. Rewrite each one to include Action, Resources, and Results.
Quantify wherever possible. Even if you weren't in a numbers-driven role, find ways to highlight your contributions—time saved, processes improved, improved customer satisfaction.
Tailor ARR Statements for Each Job. Align your accomplishments with the job description's key skills and needs.

Resumes that focus on responsibilities blend in. Resumes that highlight results stand out. The ARR Method ensures that your experience isn't just listed. It's leveraged. When hiring managers see clear, data-backed achievements, they know exactly the value you bring.

Make These Resume Fixes

Ditch the objective statement. No one cares that you're "seeking a challenging role in a dynamic company." Use that space for a strong summary that highlights your skills and impact.

Use the 15-minute resume customization rule. Before submitting your resume, scan the job description and adjust your bullet points to match the most important keywords and requirements. Don't rewrite everything. Just tweak key phrases.

Make each bullet count. Every line should pass the "So what?" test. Instead of "managed a team of five," say, "led a team of five to exceed sales targets by 20% in six months."

Cut the fluff. If a phrase doesn't add value, delete it. "Strong work ethic" and "detail-oriented" aren't achievements. Use specific, measurable results.

Test for scannability. Stop making people work to find what they need to see. Slap them in the face with it instead!

How LinkedIn Complements Your Resume

Are you sick of hearing me tell you to use LinkedIn and use terms like personal brand? TOO BAD BECAUSE I'M TRYING TO HELP YOU GET A JOB! A resume gets you in the door, but LinkedIn gets you discovered. (I'll talk about this a lot more in the next chapter.) If you only update your resume and ignore LinkedIn, you're missing out on huge opportunities. Recruiters don't just look at applications; they search for candidates on LinkedIn every.single.day. Your LinkedIn profile is not just an online resume. It's a personal branding tool for the following reasons:

It's searchable. Unlike your resume, which only gets seen when you apply, a well-optimized LinkedIn profile can get recruiters to find you first.
It's more dynamic. You're limited to one or two pages on a resume, but LinkedIn lets you expand on your achievements, post content, and engage with industry leaders.
It's proof of credibility. Your profile shows recommendations, endorsements, and real-world engagement—things a resume alone can't do.

A strong LinkedIn presence reinforces everything your resume says while opening doors your resume can't. Hiring managers and recruiters are actively searching LinkedIn. Make sure you show up. Here are the highlights:

Your headline matters more than you think. Most people just put their job title. That's a mistake. Instead of "Marketing Manager," try: "Growth-Focused Marketing Leader | Helping Brands Scale Through Data-Driven Strategy."
Use your About section wisely. This is your elevator pitch. Make it compelling, specific, and personality-driven. Highlight your biggest career wins. Feel free to use bullet points for readability. End with a call to action, for example, "Open to networking and new opportunities."
Experience section = more than just a copy-paste of your

resume. Your LinkedIn shouldn't be a carbon copy of your resume. Add depth—link to projects, articles, or case studies. Expand on how you solved problems and drove impact.
Engage to stay visible. Your profile is only as strong as your activity. Hiring managers notice candidates who comment on industry discussions, share articles or insights about their expertise, post original content, or even just short takeaways from their work.
Get recommendations and endorsements. A great LinkedIn profile has social proof. Reach out to past managers or colleagues and ask for genuine endorsements that highlight your strengths.

A Real World Success Story

Nick had been with the same company for ten years until he suddenly lost his job. His resume was a long list of buzzwords and every duty he had done over that time. He was left with four pages of generic responsibilities that he was asking hiring managers to dig through for what they cared about. Nick and I focused on a few things: We made sure the greatest value he offered was highlighted in the top third of his resume. We deleted his long list of responsibilities, focused on his most significant accomplishments, and wrote them in ARR format. We tailored his resume to speak to and target the job he wanted, not every job he's ever done. He also tailored his resume to each job posting, mirroring keywords from descriptions without stuffing them in like a desperate SEO intern.

I ran into Nick at the Chicago airport recently. We were both heading to the same place for a work trip. We caught up and discussed how the changes he made helped him in his job search and how great his new role is.

Mike's take: Nick's mistake was the same mistake most job seekers make, thinking a resume is a historical record rather than a highlight reel. Hiring managers don't have time and *won't bother* to decode your potential. If you're not showing measurable impact, they're swiping left. And yes, I included this story because I was recognized at an airport by someone I helped, and that made me feel super famous.

A strong resume gets noticed, but a strong LinkedIn gets you recruited. The best job seekers don't just apply—they build a presence. When you optimize both your resume and LinkedIn, you create a personal brand that attracts opportunities.

Mike's Snarky Do's and Don'ts of Resume Writing

DO make your resume a results-driven marketing document. Hiring managers care about impact, not responsibilities. You probably do have numbers, even if you think you don't.

DO optimize for keywords without sounding like a human thesaurus. Yes, ATS systems exist. No, "synergistically facilitated cross-functional paradigm shifts" will not impress the ATS, nor the humans. I honestly fell asleep writing that sentence.

DO tailor your resume for each job. No, you don't need to rewrite it from scratch. But tweaking keywords and bullet points for relevance? That's the move. If you spend more than 10–15 minutes tailoring a resume, you're applying for the wrong job. (Did I tell you to stop applying for the wrong jobs yet?)

DO use strong action verbs. No, you didn't help or assist. You *led*, *optimized*, *streamlined*, and *transformed*. It's okay to brag and use words that make you cringe.

DON'T include an objective statement. Every objective is the same: to get a job!

DON'T write a generic summary. I always like to say that if I can take your summary and put it on a different person's resume, then it's not a good summary. You're all data-driven team players!

DON'T cram everything onto one page just because some outdated career advice says to. Two pages are fine if you have relevant experience that strengthens your case.

DON'T forget LinkedIn. They both count and are not just carbon copies of each other.

CHAPTER THREE

A Guide to Networking & LinkedIn for Realists

TL;DR

Networking isn't some sleazy, transactional thing—it's just building real relationships over time. Most people treat networking like a last-minute job search Hail Mary, and that's why it feels awkward and doesn't work. If you only reach out when you need something, you're doing it wrong.

The truth is, networking is about staying connected, engaging naturally, and making sure you're top-of-mind when opportunities pop up. Stop sliding into DMs asking for jobs and start treating people like humans. If you network the right way—consistently, authentically, and before you need a job—you'll never have to panic network again.

Also, let's kill the myth that "most jobs aren't posted" because, surprise, they are.

Networking Is Not a Dirty Word

I hate networking. I always have. Well, I did until I actually learned how to network.

I especially hate *networking* the way many career coach gurus talk about it. For most people, networking has become a dirty word that suggests some phony interaction that feels gross and transactional.

I spent most of my career not caring about networking, and I paid the price when I really needed it the most. Most job seekers treat networking as a last resort. I sure did. They ignore peers, coworkers, mentors, topics in their industry, and anything else they could have paid attention to, and then start sending awkward LinkedIn messages or forcing themselves to go to cringeworthy networking events when they need a job. It's no wonder that people think networking doesn't work!

For the sake of simplicity, here is what networking is not:

- Messaging strangers asking about jobs
- Messaging strangers asking about referrals
- A fast way to find a job if you don't have a strong network

These things are not networking. They are cold calling. They are a part of applying for jobs, and they can work because everything can work. Cold sales outreach also sometimes works, but most of the time, it doesn't. When a salesperson has a bad day, they won't say that it was because they were trying to network and failed. They know that sales is not networking. Here's the truth about what networking actually is:

- A long-term time investment
- Making real connections with real people over real things
- Far more likely to help you on your next job search than your current one if you're just now learning what networking really is

Okay, great. We're in agreement. We're going to stop calling LinkedIn cold DMs about jobs *networking*. Since a large majority of networking for most people is limited to LinkedIn activity, I'm going to spend some time talking about how to make the most of LinkedIn as well. It's hard to separate networking from LinkedIn these days anyway. Now let's get to some networking truths.

Did you know 2397% of jobs are never posted?

You've probably heard of "the hidden job market." (I wrote that in a scary ghost voice, so please go back and read it that way.) The idea that 70% or 80% or whatever-made-up-number-it-is-today of jobs are never posted. I'll be very blunt here. Surprise! This is dumb, and I hate it every time I hear it. It doesn't even make sense on its face. According to the Bureau of Labor Statistics, there were 7.6 million jobs open in December 2024. If that represented only 20% of actual job openings, there would have been 38 million open jobs. If this were a TikTok video, I'd be giving some serious side eye. I don't care if those BLS statistics are right, close, or way off, they definitely don't represent only 20% of open jobs. Also, for what it's worth, those statistics almost always cite the same study that was done in the '80s. Personally, as someone who was alive in the '80s, I'm not sure job searching was the same then as it is now.

The truth is that a lot of jobs are filled because of networking. Right before finishing this book, I ran a few polls of a few thousand job seekers. The question was simple: How did you get your last job?

The results:

42% Application
34% Network/Referral
19% Company reached out
4% other

This is far from scientific, but it is recent data from real people with all kinds of different professional experiences. To me, there are a few big takeaways from this data, which is very similar to other recent data I've seen:

- Most people still get jobs by applying to them, despite what people tell you. Most recruiters will also tell you that the majority of their hires are from applications.
- 1/3 is no small number! It's not a majority, but you're almost as likely to get a job by networking as by applying, so no more excuses for only applying and not networking.
- Almost 20% of hires were made as a result of the company reaching out, so I repeat: YOUR LinkedIn MATTERS!

If you're only applying to jobs online, you're playing with a stacked deck—and not in your favor. Networking isn't optional. Don't just apply. The best strategy is to do everything people do to get hired, and that includes taking the time to network. It may not help you today, but you'll thank me for this on your next job search!

The Anti-Cringe Approach to Networking

Networking gets a bad rap because most people do it wrong. They wait until they need a job, then frantically start cold-messaging strangers or showing up at networking events like a lost puppy. That's not networking. It's panic. And panic smells desperate.

The biggest mistake job seekers make is treating networking as a last-minute job search hack instead of what it actually is: relationship building. If you only reach out to people when you need something, you're setting yourself up for awkward interactions. Think about it. If an old friend texts you out of the blue asking for a favor, your first thought is, *Really? Now, you reach out?*

Instead, networking should be an ongoing, low-pressure habit. It's not about asking for a job. It's about staying connected with people, so opportunities come to you naturally. You have to build relationships over time and anticipate that results won't be instant. Even my best friend can't just get me a job tomorrow, but I'll be the first person they think of when they hear about an opportunity.

The Biggest Networking Myths (And Why They're Wrong)

Myth: "I don't have a network."
Reality: You do—former coworkers, classmates, friends, even people you randomly talk to at events.
Myth: "Networking means schmoozing at happy hours."
Reality: No, it means engaging in meaningful conversations—online or offline.
Myth: "I'm not an extrovert, so I'm bad at networking."
Reality: Introverts often excel at networking because they focus on building deeper, quality connections. Just like job applications, it's not a numbers game of how many people you can connect with. It's how many great connections you can make.

The Networking Rule of Three: A Simple Habit for Career Growth

Networking works when it's steady and sustainable. That's where the Networking Rule of Three comes in. Three small actions, done consistently, can keep your network engaged without making you feel like a sleazy salesperson.

Reconnect with one old contact per week. Send a casual check-in to a former coworker, a past manager, or an industry peer you haven't spoken to in a while.
Engage with three industry posts per week. Comment on LinkedIn, reply to online discussions, or contribute to a Slack group. The key is visibility.
Reach out to one new person per week. A new LinkedIn connection, a warm intro from a mutual contact, or a quick message to someone whose work you admire.

The key to networking isn't grand gestures. It's small, consistent touchpoints that keep you top of mind. Hiring decisions happen year-round, and staying visible means you'll be the first person people think of when an opportunity pops up. Sometimes these conversations may only be one line long, and then you don't speak again for a while, and that's ok. Stop putting so much pressure on every interaction, and just start treating people like people.

The Give-Before-You-Ask Networking Mindset

The best networkers don't show up just when they need something—they add value first. This makes networking feel organic instead of transactional. Ways to do this:

- Share an interesting article with someone in your industry.
- Comment on LinkedIn posts with thoughtful insights. Don't just say, "Great post!"
- Congratulate people on new jobs, promotions, or achievements.
- Offer to introduce people who could benefit from knowing each other.
- Provide a quick tip or resource relevant to their work.
- Recognize and highlight people's contributions in discussions or group settings. When you invest in your professional relationships *before you need anything*, reaching out for help later feels natural, not desperate or transactional.

Networking does feel sleazy when it's purely transactional—when people only reach out because they need something. You know the type: the person who hasn't spoken to you in five years but suddenly appears in your inbox with "Hey! Hope you're well. Also, I'm job hunting—any leads?" Yeah, don't be that person.

The trick to non-cringey networking? Give before you ask. Relationships built on genuine interaction lead to long-term opportunities, not just one-time favors. Instead of diving straight into someone's messages begging for a job, start by engaging with them first. Comment on their LinkedIn post, share their content, or respond to something insightful they've written. People remember engagement more than a cold DM.

Once you're ready to reach out, make the conversation about them, not just you. Instead of "Can you help me find a job?" try something more thoughtful: "I really admire the work you're doing at [company]. I'd love to hear how you approached [specific challenge or project]." This shifts the focus from a transactional ask to an organic conversation. When people feel like you value their expertise, they're far more likely to help.

Following up naturally is the key to keeping relationships warm. If you only reach out when you need something, you're a user, not a connector. A simple "Hope you're doing well!" or "Saw this article and thought of you" keeps you on their radar without being overbearing. Good networking is about long-term investment, not short-term gains. The strongest professional relationships aren't forced; they're built through consistent, thoughtful interactions over time.

The simplest tip of all is this little off-the-wall idea? Try talking to people about anything but work! In-person networking events feel gross and fake because most people at them act fake. I am constantly asked about how to make more of these opportunities. And the answer is… drumroll, please… to stop talking about work, especially as a conversation starter.

Conversations that lead with questions like "What do you do?" are bound to end quickly and with no real connection. Instead, try talking about LITERALLY ANYTHING ELSE. Talk about the venue, the food and drink, or that funny thing that happened this morning. Talk about your favorite TV show or hobby. Talk about anything. And eventually, maybe you'll get around to work. I've said it before, and I'll say it again: try treating people like people!

Not All Connections Are Created Equal

Just as you wouldn't ask a stranger for a huge favor or treat a close friend like a random LinkedIn acquaintance, how you leverage your network—what you can ask for and from whom—depends on where each connection falls on this spectrum. Here is a helpful way to think about reaching out to connect.

A Cold Contact: Someone you've never spoken to before but admire professionally. You need a shared interest or mutual connection to start a real conversation.

A Warm Contact: Someone you've engaged with in some way—commented on their posts, met at a conference, or exchanged a couple of LinkedIn messages.

A Hot Contact: Someone you have an actual relationship with—maybe a former coworker, mentor, or someone you've had multiple conversations with.

Cold contacts require an introduction or common ground before they'll be open to helping you. Warm contacts need a clear reason for your outreach, while hot contacts can handle a direct but strategic job-related ask.

But let's face it. Some people are just never going to respond to you, but also don't you dare sit there reading this book pretending that you respond to every text, DM, and email you get either! Life happens, and people are busy. You may have trouble believing this, but you are not the main character of everyone's story. Sometimes, they do not mean to ignore you, sometimes they can't help you, but it doesn't mean they are not interested.

Here are some tips to try to engage with people you really want to engage with who seem not to be reciprocating without feeling like a pest:

Use the touchpoint rule. Every four to six months, find a reason to check in. Comment on a post, share an article, or congratulate them on something.

Make it about them. Instead of "Can you help me?" try, "Hey, I saw this article and thought of you. I'd love to hear what you think."

Avoid generic messages. No more "Just checking in!" Instead, reference a conversation or recent event to restart the dialogue naturally.

Leverage shared interests. People are more likely to respond if you share something of interest in common. Work in the same industry? Follow the same influencers? Bring it up.

Be authentic. The best networking is natural, not scripted. Talk to people the way you'd want someone to talk to you.

A Real World Success Story

A product manager had no plans to switch jobs but liked to engage on LinkedIn now and then. One of the people they interacted with? A former boss who had moved on to a different company. Instead of sending an awkward "Hope you're doing well. Also, I need a job" message, they simply liked and commented on their old boss's posts from time to time. Then, one day, the boss reached out first, "Hey, we're growing our team, and I think you'd be a perfect fit. Let's talk."

Mike's take: They never had to ask. By staying visible without being pushy, they positioned themselves as a top choice when the right opportunity opened up.

Networking isn't about chasing people down and asking for favors. It's about building relationships, staying visible, and knowing how to ask for help the right way. If you approach your network strategically—by adding value, staying in touch, and making it easy for others to help—you won't just get job leads. You'll have a network that actively works for you.

The Ask Without Asking Strategy

Nobody likes getting a message that says, "Hey, do you know of any job openings?" It puts the other person in an awkward position and makes them feel pressured to do your homework for you. Instead, shift the conversation to make them want to help. Instead of "Can you help me find a job?" Try: "I'm exploring new opportunities in [industry]. Do you have any advice for someone looking to break into [specific type of role]?" or "I've always admired how [their company] approaches [specific industry challenge]. Any advice on how someone like me could add value at a company like yours?" These approaches do two things: they open up the conversation instead of shutting it down, and they give the other person the chance to offer help on their terms. And if they don't, that's okay too. Just like job applications, you are going to have a lot more failures than successes, but it doesn't mean you don't keep trying.

A Real World Success Story

Christine was searching for a job, and a video of hers popped up on my page as I was scrolling through TikTok. She was on a rant about recruiters and how bad they are. I wrote an honest comment to try to explain some of what was behind some of her frustrations on the recruiter side, and we had a positive conversation and began to follow each other. I wanted to watch her job search journey.

Over the next month or two, we started engaging more in each other's content and getting to know each other a bit better. We also then moved our relationship over to LinkedIn connections. Gag. From there, we would exchange messages now and then about the tech industry, recruiting, her job search, her living in an area close to where I grew up, kids, all kinds of things. We were people treating people like people.

Soon a personal connection of mine posted about a job they were hiring for on LinkedIn, and Christine was the first person I thought of. I connected the two of them, told them they should talk, and a few weeks later, Christine had a new job. A few months later, we even got to meet IRL for coffee when I was in her city!

Mike's take: This is real networking. This is why I LOVE real networking. Christine is now a lifelong friend, and I was glad to eventually introduce her to the right person to get her a great job. She never asked me for a job. We didn't have to talk every day. We didn't chase a transactional relationship. We simply treated each other like people, and when the time was right, she was the person I thought of.

You can do this. You already do it more than you realize. You just don't think of it as networking yet. But it is.

How to Keep Networking Without Burning Out

Most people assume networking means hours of forced conversations and awkward follow-ups. It doesn't. It means being strategic, efficient, and consistent.

Batch your efforts. Spend 10–15 minutes twice a week engaging on LinkedIn instead of scrambling when you need a job.
Use reminders. Set a calendar alert every few months to check in with key contacts. If you wait until you "remember," you won't do it.
Automate what you can. Use LinkedIn's "keep in touch" feature or set up simple CRM reminders to track who you've engaged with.
Be selective. Not every connection is worth maintaining. Focus on quality, not quantity.
Most people love talking about their experiences, especially when they feel like they are being genuinely engaged and not like they're being used. The key is to approach networking as a conversation, not a transaction.
Keep it light. Don't come in with a huge ask right away.
Find a reason to reach out. It could be a shared interest, a mutual connection, or even a recent industry trend.
Make it about them. Ask questions, be genuinely curious, and show appreciation.

Follow up strategically. Don't just disappear after one conversation. Check in occasionally, share something relevant, or even just say, "Hope you're doing well!"
Be patient. Building relationships takes time. You wouldn't expect instant results in friendships, so don't expect it in networking.

Networking doesn't have to feel sleazy, forced, or cringey. When done right, it's just building relationships, staying visible, and being helpful. If you approach networking as a long-term investment rather than a last-minute scramble, opportunities will come to you—not the other way around.

LinkedIn is More Than an Online Resume

Remember that 19% of hires are made by the company reaching out from a few pages ago? Recruiters don't use LinkedIn the way job seekers do. They're not scrolling through pages of applications; they're searching for candidates. I mean literally opening up LinkedIn Recruiter, which you don't have access to, and typing in skills, job titles, and keywords to see who shows up. If your profile is sitting dormant, they're not going to find you. You're not popping. A strong LinkedIn profile isn't about listing jobs you've had—it's about search engine optimization and branding yourself as someone worth hiring. How do you do this?

Optimize your profile. Your headline, About section, and experience need to do more than just list your past jobs. They should communicate who you are, what you do, and why you're valuable.
Share content and engage. Commenting on posts, sharing insights, and engaging with industry leaders make you visible. The best candidates don't just apply—they get noticed. Did you know that when you engage with content a company posts and a recruiter runs their LinkedIn search, you show up in a different tab? That's the tab they often start with when looking at candidates to reach out to.

Network. You don't need to "network" in the traditional sense, but engaging with people in your industry keeps you top of mind. Nearly all of my networking tips can be applied to LinkedIn as well. You can also mark companies you are interested in on their About pages, which yet again puts you on a different list when recruiters from that company search on LinkedIn.

Fix Your LinkedIn Profile to Attract Opportunities

Your headline is prime real estate. "Marketing Manager" is forgettable. "Data-Driven Marketer | Helping SaaS Startups Scale with Performance Campaigns" stands out. Your About section should tell a story, not be a list. Make it engaging, highlight wins, and make it easy to skim. Your experience section should show your impact, not just your duties. Use the ARR Method (Action, Resources, Results) here, the same as on your resume.

Here is how to optimize each section of your profile:

Headline: Go beyond just your title. Think of it as your personal brand statement. Example: "Customer Success Leader | Reducing Churn & Scaling Client Retention by 40%"
About Section: Write it in the first person, make it conversational, and highlight your unique skills, achievements, and career story.
Experience Section: Treat this as an achievement list, not a task list. Show measurable impact with percentages, revenue growth, and process improvements.
Skills & Endorsements: List industry-relevant skills, and get colleagues to endorse them. The more endorsements, the more visible you are in search results.
Recommendations: Ask past managers or coworkers for short, meaningful recommendations that endorse your expertise.

The LinkedIn Content Playbook

Posting daily isn't necessary, but engagement is. Commenting on industry posts, asking smart questions, and sharing insights keep you in front of the right people. Not sure what to post? Try:

- Lessons learned from a recent project
- Thoughts on industry trends
- A resource or article that changed how you work
- A brief story about overcoming a professional challenge
- Insights from an event or webinar you attended
- A simple here's-what-I-learned takeaway from your daily work
- A success story or a small win you achieved. You don't have to be an influencer—you just have to be visible.

Smart LinkedIn Networking Without Feeling Weird

Most people think networking means sending random connection requests with an "I'd love to connect!" message. Try any or all of these instead:

Comment first. Before connecting, engage with a person's posts.
Personalize requests. "Hey [Name], I loved your post on [topic]. I'd love to stay connected and follow more of your work."
Start conversations. Instead of "Can you help me get a job?" say literally anything else! I couldn't even think of a better quote to write here because anything would be better!
Engaging with recruiters the right way. Comment on their posts, message with a specific question about a role, and build a rapport over time. DO NOT MESSAGE THEM ASKING IF THEY HAVE ANY JOBS FOR YOU!
Join relevant industry groups and participate in discussions. Hiring managers and recruiters often look for candidates engaged in these spaces. There are people just like you

in these groups who are also looking to get to know you.
Share others' successes. If a colleague posts about a big win, comment, congratulate them, and add your own thoughts. It strengthens connections and keeps you top of mind.

The keyword in all of this is authenticity. If you don't want to feel phony, then don't be phony. Just treat people like people!

Real World Wins

If you don't follow me on LinkedIn, first of all, HOW DARE YOU? Second, you're missing real-world daily proof that you can be yourself and still succeed on that platform. While other people may be posting inspirational quotes on billboards or made-up stories about rescuing a dog who was actually the CEO, I'm busy posting things like magic tricks, videos of a camera falling on me in a TikTok outtake, or coloring book pages I made of tech bros taking 5 AM ice baths. (Yes, I actually posted all these things on LinkedIn.) But you know what? It works. The people who I want to find me and engage with me do, and I try to get to know them too. I have landed jobs, consulting gigs, brand deals, media articles, podcast invites, and more just by doing LinkedIn the way I wanted to.

Networking isn't about begging for jobs or forcing awkward conversations. It's about showing up, staying visible, and building the genuine relationships that you want to build over time. If you start before you need a job, you'll never have to "network" in desperation mode.

Your LinkedIn presence should make it easy for recruiters to find you, easy for connections to engage with you, and easy for hiring managers to see why you're valuable. Stop treating LinkedIn like an afterthought. Almost everybody who tells me LinkedIn is useless and has never helped them is simply checking a box by being on there. They are using it as nothing more than a job search board and then wondering why it doesn't work.

Yes, there are a lot of people doing a lot of cringey things on LinkedIn, but also, have you checked any other social media platform recently? Because…well, I'll let you explore for yourself!

MIKE'S SNARKY DO'S AND DON'TS OF JOB SEARCHING

DO build relationships before you need them. If the first time you reach out to someone is when you're job hunting, you're already behind.

DO offer value first. Comment on posts, share useful insights, and be the person who helps before they ask for help.

DO be consistent. Networking isn't about one big ask. It's about small, strategic touchpoints over time.

DO be specific when reaching out. "Would love to pick your brain" is vague and overused.

DO follow up. A simple "Hope you're doing well!" or "Saw this article and thought of you" keeps relationships warm.

DON'T treat networking like a last-minute life raft. If you only reach out when you need something, you're doing it wrong.

DON'T send generic LinkedIn connection requests. If you can't be bothered to add a personal note, don't expect a reply.

DON'T expect instant results. Relationships take time. The best job referrals come from ongoing connections, not random messages from strangers.

DON'T be weird about it. If someone doesn't respond, move on.

DON'T fall for the made-up stats. Networking is a huge part of finding a job, but it is not the only way, and there are not eleventy billion hidden jobs. (I forget what number I said at the beginning of the chapter, and don't feel like scrolling back up).

Networking isn't about begging for jobs. It's about building real relationships that lead to real opportunities. Play the long game, stay visible, and make sure people think of you first when the right job opens up.

CHAPTER FOUR

Why Cold Outreach Works (And Doesn't)

TL;DR

Cold outreach has a bad reputation, and a lot of it is well deserved. Most people hate doing it, assume it doesn't work, and give up after getting no response. But here's the truth: cold outreach can work when it's done right. The problem isn't the concept; it's the execution. Sending a generic "Hi, I'd love to connect!" message to a stranger won't get you very far. But a thoughtful, personal, and valuable message that actually gives someone a reason to respond? That can move you from the bottom of the resume pile straight to a hiring manager's inbox.

In this chapter, we're going to break down how to craft cold outreach messages that actually get noticed, how to follow up without sounding desperate, and how to guide a casual response into a real opportunity. We'll look at what makes messages stand out, the biggest mistakes job seekers make, and why "spray and pray" is not a strategy. Cold outreach isn't magic, but it is a skill, and if you're going to try it, let's make sure you do it well.

Cold Outreach Can Work, When Done Right

We have already covered that cold outreach and networking are not the same thing. Hopefully, you noticed that I did not say that you shouldn't do cold outreach! I just want you to stop calling it *networking!* Most job seekers hate cold outreach because they assume it doesn't work. And they're not totally wrong because it doesn't work more often than it does. But the problem isn't cold outreach itself. It's how people do it. If done correctly, cold outreach isn't just effective; it can bump you to the top of a pile. Think about it. If cold outreach didn't work, why are there still 239923908* salespeople in your email every day? A well-crafted outreach message isn't about just asking for a job; it's about showing somebody how you can be a valuable part of their team.

Hiring managers and recruiters are flooded with boring, boilerplate messages every.single.day. If your outreach looks like everyone else's, it has a higher chance of being ignored. People respond to messages that feel personal, intentional, and valuable. They are more likely to respond to the kind of message that stands out from the bad outreach they see every day. This is why a warm, personalized, and engaging message will be far more effective than a generic job request.

That said, you could send a great message that will never be read despite its obvious brilliance. Consider that, as a recruiter, I sometimes receive several hundred emails about a single job. It would be unrealistic to expect me to read and reply to every one, on top of actually reviewing the resumes and doing all the other parts of my job. Accepting this is important because a complaint I often hear is "nobody responds to my messages."

Despite what some content creators will tell you, reaching out to managers and recruiters is not a secret hack. But it is one more tool to try that may or may not work for you. However, if you are going to do it, you might as well do it well. So let's talk about that.

Let's be clear: Cold outreach is not a numbers game. Many job seekers figure that if they send enough messages, eventually, something will stick. That's why hiring managers get flooded with boring, generic, and downright cringeworthy messages that

*Number not researched!

they will simply ignore without hesitation. If your outreach looks just like everyone else's, it will be ignored. What is the difference between a cold message that sparks a conversation and one that vanishes into the abyss? Thought, strategy, and a clear reason to engage.

The Structure of a Winning Cold Outreach Message

The best cold outreach doesn't feel cold; it feels like a natural extension of a conversation. People respond to messages that feel personal, intentional, and valuable. A well-written message should make the recipient think that the writer actually put in effort. A great message is concise, makes the recipient feel valued, and provides an easy and obvious reason to respond.

Subject Line: This is the first thing they see, and it needs to stand out. Make it personal and relevant. "I loved your take on [industry topic]—quick question!"
Opening Line: The biggest mistake? Leading with your ask. Instead, start by mentioning something specific about *them, their* work, company, project, or post. Cringe all you like, but a little flattery tends to work best.
Value Proposition: Why are you reaching out? Instead of making it about you, show how you relate to their work, company, or expertise.
A Clear Call to Action (CTA): A weak message ends with "Would love to connect!" A strong one gives a low-pressure next step. But remember, if your request sounds like work, they won't respond. Keep it easy. Here are a couple of options:
Curiosity Hook: Ask a question they will want to answer, something they're already thinking about. Try, "I would love to hear your perspective on [relevant topic] when you have a moment." Be genuine.
Low Commitment Ask: Instead of "Do you have any remote roles?" try, "I saw you are hiring a remote [position], is that something you're directly overseeing?"

SIDEBAR

Wait a second. Did I just say to provide a value prop in these messages? Who do I think I am with that kind of garbage? You're already begging them for attention, and now I'm telling you that if you make it too much about you, they won't even respond? I get it. But the issue is probably me using corporate-speak instead of really just being totally blunt about what I mean. People are busy, and people are inherently selfish. If your message doesn't make clear how they are going to be better off because they replied to your message, why should they reply? Imagine a world where you posted on LinkedIn (or wherever you feel less cringe about posting) that you need a new bike. And then, after your post, you get 400 offers from people who have the *perfect* bike for you. You haven't asked these people to beg you for attention, and you're far more likely to reply to the messages that make clear why their bike is actually the right bike for you. It may feel disingenuous or slimy or whatever else, but substitute the high-stakes idea of job searching with any other scenario, and this will still be obvious. So once again, I implore you just to write the message properly and stop worrying about whether you should even have to do it. I'll even show you how I do it!

Common Cold Outreach Mistakes (And How to Avoid Them)

Mistake	Why It Fails	The Fix
Using a generic template	"Hi, I'd love to connect!" screams spam.	Personalize based on their work, company, or interests.
Asking them to do the work	"I'm looking for a job. Can you help?" pressures the recipient to figure out how to help.	Reach out with a specific purpose. "I saw this job on your website. I would be a great fit..."
Sending a massive block of text	No one wants to read a novel from a stranger.	Keep it short, direct, and skimmable.
Making it all about you	"I'm looking for a job. Can you help?" is all about you.	Make the conversation about them first. What do they do? What do they care about?
Not showing your value	This is your chance to sell them on you. Don't just ask for help.	Highlight how your skills and experience align with the job you are messaging about.
Using a generic template	"Hi, I'd love to connect!" is meaningless.	Write customized messages based on their background or the job.
No Call To Action	You got their attention and then did nothing with it.	Wrap up your message with a clear CTA, whether requesting a conversation, sharing your portfolio, or asking about next steps.
Not Following Up	People are busy and forget to reply.	Send a strategic follow-up that adds value instead of just checking in.

Here are some basic templates of good examples of short and direct cold outreach messages, of what this should look like in the wild:

> **Good Example:** "Hi [Name], I read your post about [topic]. It was really insightful. I'm currently working on something similar at [company] and would love to hear your perspective. Would you be open to a quick chat?"
>
> **Good Example:** "Hey [Name], I saw your team is hiring. Your approach to [industry challenge] really resonated with me. I would love to talk more about how I took on a similar challenge in my previous role, where I did [value add]. I'd love to chat a bit more about the open role. Do you have a preferred way of setting up a time to discuss?"

And here are some examples of what not to do. Don't be this guy.

> **Bad Example:** "Hi [Name], I'm looking for opportunities in [industry]. Let me know if you know of anything!"
>
> **Bad Example:** "Hi [Name], I came across your profile and wanted to connect!"

Mike's Successful Outreach Story

Did you know I got laid off? Have I ever mentioned it? Well, boy, was I in a funk in November of 2022 as Thanksgiving approached. I felt like my career had hit its bottom. But then I saw a job that felt like a perfect fit for me. It was at a similar-sized company and in the same niche industry as the job from which I'd just been let go. And I wanted it!

First, I researched the company, and I learned about the product and the team. I learned about the challenges they were currently facing, and I dug into why they were hiring a recruiter right at that moment. Here is the exact message I sent. And yes, I'm aware that it doesn't follow every piece of my own advice! Let that make the point that there is no magical template or rules you have to follow. Note that it absolutely did follow the most important pieces of advice.

> *I know in this crazy market with hundreds of applications what your inbox looks like this evening, but I was REALLY interested in [Company] after reading more about the [specific project] and needed to at least try to climb to the top of the pile. I want to be brief, out of respect, but here are some reasons this feels like a good fit to me: I have led teams while being a hands-on recruiter in small, highly technical startup environments. My latest company was an under-50-person San Francisco-based open-source security company with a very high technical bar that is just close enough to a competitor to not be a problem. Beyond that, I am the kind of employee that any company would be proud to have as its public face and the first person that future employees meet. I want to build a great company from the early stages.*
>
> *I did not plan to be on the job market, and my last C.E.O. was clear on LinkedIn that given the opportunity, with a stronger economic outlook, they would bring me back to continue building. But now that I am on the market, [specific project] SCREAMS at me to bug you with this message, despite the odds!*
>
> *I do hope you get to see this and that we can speak soon.*

An hour later, their hiring manager responded, "Thanks for your note, Mike. Just sent you an email. :)" That email was an interview request. Cold outreach isn't about begging for a job. It's about starting conversations that lead to opportunities. If you make the message about more than just needing a job, provide value, and make it easy for them to say yes, you won't just get more responses, you'll build relationships that actually help your career.

Who Do You Reach Out To?

If you already think you have the who figured out, you can skip ahead to the next section about how to follow up, but if you have no idea who the recipients should be of your brilliant, short, direct cold outreach emails with their clear calls to action, then this section is for you.

Whether your cold-outreach email gets read and responded to is not only a function of its personalized contents; it's also a function of whether you send it to the right address. I don't mean email address, but yes, that too. I mean to the right person. Messaging the wrong people wastes time, energy, and opportunities. If you're reaching out to HR or to a generic "careers@" email, you're setting yourself up for disappointment. The key to effective cold outreach is targeting the right people. Who are they? The people who actually have the power to open doors for you. Your best targets for cold outreach are:

Hiring Managers and Recruiters: The decision-makers who actually have the power to bring you in for an interview.
Team Members (Future Peers): Employees working in the role you want who can provide insider information and internal referrals.
Industry Peers & Thought Leaders: Engaging with people who are active in your space builds credibility and future opportunities.
Alumni & Mutual Connections: People with shared backgrounds (same schools or previous workplaces) are more likely to respond.

Cold outreach isn't just about crafting the right message; it's about sending it to the right person. You maximize your chances of getting a response by targeting hiring managers, future peers, and warm connections. The best outreach isn't about spraying and praying. It's about strategic targeting that puts you ahead of the competition.

How to Follow Up Without Being a Pest (and a Half)

Most job seekers struggle with follow-ups because they assume that no response is itself a rejection. So they either never follow up at all, or (worse!) they send generic "just checking in" emails that make them look desperate. The reality? There are any number of reasons a person doesn't respond. They're busy, and your message got buried under 100 others. Remember what I said in the networking chapter about treating people like people? Every single one of you reading this book (I hope people are reading this book!) has at some point forgotten to reply to an email, text, or phone call. I know it! You looked at it, didn't reply right away, said you'd do it later, and then you didn't. People are people. So if you've done it before and had no ill intent, it's only fair to assume that so has everyone else. They forgot. Their non-response wasn't intentional; it just slipped through the cracks. They may not have an answer for you yet. Hiring processes take weeks, sometimes months.

Did your message give them a reason to respond? If your follow-up was just "checking in," it's not adding value and so may not merit a response. Most people don't respond to the first message, not because they're not interested but because they're busy. But sending a bland reminder misses the point. A well-crafted follow-up shows persistence without desperation and can make the difference between being forgotten and getting hired.

Follow-Up Strategy: What to Do When You Don't Get a Response

Repeat after me: *I will never send more than three emails to another human without getting any response.* Say it again. And again. In this case, we'll start with the don't-dos, and then we'll talk about how to follow up professionally by adding value and keeping all the doors open for whatever possibilities the future may bring.

I swear by a Three Message Rule for cold outreach. Earlier in this chapter, we went over the rules for that first cold outreach email. It was personalized, values-driven, and had a clear CTA. Odds are pretty good that you haven't received a response not because you didn't write a great email but because a lot of cold-outreach emails don't even get read. If you want to be the person who shows persistence-but-not-desperation, it's time to learn how to write the follow-up.

If your initial outreach is met with radio silence, three to seven days later, it will be time to deploy a follow-up. But here's the rule: add value, don't nag. Your follow-up should make the recipient's life better in some way—easier, more interesting, or more engaging. Forget the bland "Just checking in" messages that scream desperation. Instead, craft a light reminder that comes packaged with something worthwhile.

The ideal first follow-up pairs a gentle nudge with a genuine insight. Something like, "Hey Jamie, hope you're doing well! Just following up on my last message. By the way, I noticed your company just launched that new [x] initiative. I'm so impressed! I would love to hear your thoughts on how that's changing your approach to [y]." This shows you're paying attention to their world and that you're not just focused on your own needs. I even used to attach kid or dog photos to follow-ups with a line like "maybe you just dislike people, but could never ignore a dog," or "Please don't make me be as desperate for an answer as my son was to eat his cake in this picture!" And like it or not, those got responses way more often!

There are several effective approaches to adding value to your follow-ups:

The Insight Follow-Up. Share an article, podcast, or industry trend that connects to their work. "Hey Taylor, I came across this fascinating piece on [x] and immediately thought about the [y] your team announced last quarter. I'd be curious if you're experiencing challenges similar to [z] as a result?" This demonstrates that you're thinking about their specific situation, not just forwarding random content.

The Progress Update Approach. If they've previously offered advice or insights, let them know how you've applied it. "Hey Morgan, I wanted to share that I took your suggestion about [x] to heart and did [y]. It's been incredibly enlightening. I wanted to say thanks and let you know it's made a real difference in how I'm [z]."

The Social Proof Approach. This one can also be effective, especially when trying to build credibility. Reference a mutual connection or engage with content they've shared. "Hey Casey, I noticed your comment on that LinkedIn thread about [x]—your point about [y] really resonated. I'd love to hear more about how you think about [z]."

Remember that the purpose of the value-add follow-up isn't just to get a response; it's to build a relationship by consistently demonstrating that you're thoughtful, attentive, and generous with your insights. People respond to people who make them think, not those who make them feel obligated.

If your value-add follow-up still doesn't get a response, it is time to gracefully move on with a short, polite message that leaves the door open for future conversations. "No worries if now isn't a great time. I would love to stay in touch." (Translation: I can take a hint, but I'm professionally persistent). Close the loop, but keep the door open. "Hey [Name], totally understand if now isn't the right time. I'd still love to stay in touch—if there's a better time to connect down the road, just let me know!" If someone doesn't respond after three attempts, it's time to shift focus to other contacts.

Following up is about building relationships, not sending reminders. A great follow-up isn't just another ping. It's a value-add that keeps the conversation moving. If you do it right, you have better odds of getting a response, and you'll be well on the way to building a network that will work for you.

Turning a Follow-Up into a Real Opportunity

Most people assume the hard part of cold outreach is getting a response. But even when someone replies, most conversations go nowhere because job seekers don't know how to guide the discussion toward a real opportunity. Sure, getting a response is step one, but turning that response into an actual job lead is where the real fun begins. There are three stages of a follow-up conversation:

The Casual Engagement Stage. You've gotten a response, but it's vague or polite. They said, "Thanks for reaching out," or "I appreciate the message." At this stage, your goal isn't to ask for a job; it's just to keep the conversation moving.

The Interest Testing Stage. You've added value, and they start asking about your background or experience. This is where you subtly align your skills with their hiring needs.

The Opportunity Window Stage. They mention an upcoming role, a hiring need, or introduce you to someone internally. This is where you pivot to the next step.

A cold outreach message should never lead with, "Are you hiring?" But once a connection has been established, you need to transition from casual conversation to job opportunity. Here's how:

Strategy	Why It Works	Example
Soft Ask Approach	Instead of "Are you hiring?" ask about their team's needs.	"I love what your team is doing with [specific project]. What skills are you looking for in future hires?"
Set a Future Touch-point	If no immediate roles are available, secure a follow-up.	"I totally understand. I'd love to check back in a few months."

You'll be able to sense that the conversation may be moving toward an opportunity when any of the following happen:

- They ask about your experience or availability.
- They introduce you to another hiring manager or recruiter.
- They mention an upcoming role or say, "We're planning to hire soon."
- They say, "Send me your resume," or "Let me put you in touch with someone."
- They start selling the company to you, talking about culture, benefits, and why people love working there.

You're getting all the good vibes. Don't screw this up. Once a hiring manager or recruiter starts giving you real signals—looking deeply into your eyes—you need to shift gears. Here are some suggestions:

- "That sounds really interesting. What's been the biggest challenge in finding the right person for that role?" (This keeps them talking and lets you position yourself as the solution.)
- "I'd love to throw my hat in the ring. What would be the best way to move forward?" (Polite but direct.)
- "Would it be helpful if I sent over my resume and a few projects I've worked on?" (This makes it easy for them to take the next step.)

Case Study: The Follow-Up That Turned a Casual Chat into a Job Offer

A marketing strategist I worked with wanted to break into a high-growth startup but had no direct connections. Instead of applying blindly, she sent a cold outreach message via LinkedIn to the VP of Marketing:

"Hey [VP's Name], I loved your recent post on [industry top-

ic]—really insightful! I've worked on similar challenges at [previous company], and I'd love to hear your thoughts on [specific issue]. No ask—just genuinely curious about your take!"

The VP actually responded. They had a quick back-and-forth discussion, but no job was mentioned. Most people would leave it at that. She didn't.

Follow-up #1: A week later, my client sent this short message:

"Hey [VP's Name], I came across this case study on [related challenge] and thought of our chat. Curious if your team has tackled something similar?"

Again, no job ask—just value. This time, the VP replied with a longer response, explaining how their team was struggling with scaling paid ads.

Follow-up #2: She saw her opportunity:

"That's a challenge I love working on. I optimized ad spend at [previous company] and increased conversions by 32%. Would love to share insights if helpful—no pressure, just happy to chat!"

Boom. She got a call the next day. The VP wasn't hiring yet, but after talking, they realized they needed someone like her. A month later, they created a role just for my client.

Mike's take: This is how you guide a conversation into an opportunity. She didn't start with "Are you hiring?" She built trust, added value, and made them realize they needed her before they even had a job posting. If you do this right, you don't chase jobs. Jobs chase you.

Turning a cold outreach response into a real job opportunity isn't about luck. It's about guiding the conversation in the right direction. If you know how to read the signals, ask the right questions, and follow up strategically, you can turn a simple reply into your next job offer.

Mike's Snarky Do's and Don'ts of Cold Outreach

DO research before reaching out. If your message could be sent to any company, it's generic and useless. Be specific.

DO keep it short and direct. No one wants to read a novel from a stranger. Your message should be under 100 words.

DO personalize, but don't be creepy. "I saw you were at Starbucks at 2:43 PM on Tuesday—want to chat?" is not the move.

DO follow up strategically. If they don't reply, give them space, add value, and try again later.

DO treat networking as a long game. The best opportunities come from relationships you've nurtured, not desperate one-off messages.

DON'T send copy-paste messages. "Hi, I'd love to connect!" gets ignored 99% of the time.

DON'T ask for a job in the first message. Build a connection first. Nobody hires a stranger from a cold DM.

DON'T write a message that's all about you. Make it about them, their work, their company, their industry.

DON'T expect instant results. Some responses take time, and some people will never reply. That's fine. Keep moving.

DON'T follow up like they owe you a reply. One reminder is fine. Three unanswered messages? Move on.

Cold outreach isn't about begging for jobs. It's about starting conversations that grow into opportunities. If you do it right, you won't just get replies. You'll build connections that actually help your career.

CHAPTER FIVE

Mike's Guide to Job Interviews

TL;DR

Stop begging for jobs and start evaluating companies. Interviews are mutual assessments. You're deciding if they deserve your talent just as much as they're deciding if they want you. This chapter shows you how to research strategically, spot genuine red flags, handle tough questions, and make hiring managers remember you when it matters.

INTERVIEW TO GET THE JOB

I've been waiting for this! Those first few chapters were fine. You already bought the book, so I can say that. But now, we're going to get into my favorite thing to talk about: job interviews! As much as I hate talking about resumes, I love talking about job interviews! Not because I'm some kind of weirdo, but because job interviews are the moment in the job search process when you start having some control over what happens the rest of the way. It's still only some, but it's better than none!

Interviewing is a skill that you can learn, practice, and improve! That sentence probably made some of you mad, so if you need to, keep reading it until it doesn't make you mad anymore, because this is one of those accept-the-way-it-is moments! I can't make the job search process not suck, I can't make untrained interviewers stop existing, and I can't make everyone stop asking stupid questions. But what I can do, by the end of these next few chapters, is help you be the kind of candidate companies want to hire, or at least teach you how to walk that walk. It's time to start interviewing to get the job and to stop interviewing not to lose the job.

HOW TO RESEARCH A COMPANY IN TEN MINUTES AND ACTUALLY LEARN SOMETHING USEFUL

Interview prep isn't like cramming for a high school history test—memorizing company facts, skimming the "About Us" page, and hoping you can bluff your way through. Knowing the company's founding year doesn't tell you if you actually want to work there. Interview prep isn't just about impressing the company; it's about figuring out if this company fits your career goals as well. Before you walk into an interview, you need to answer two questions:

1. What do I need to know to position myself as the best candidate?
2. What do I need to know to decide if this company is worth my time?

Hiring managers don't care if you know when the company was founded or who the CEO is (unless that CEO is sitting across from you in the interview). They care if you understand the company's challenges, values, and priorities. They want to see that you've thought about how you would fit into their world, not just that you can parrot back a mission statement.

Forget endless Google searches. Here's how to extract real insights fast:

Step 1: Start On the Company Website

- Read the company values. These are magic buzzwords in the interview. Whether you think companies live by their values or not, they believe they do, and they are proud of them. Any chance you get to drop these values into your interview helps. You will also come up with questions based on these for later.
- Look at the company's News page. This may be called something different, but most companies have a page bragging about what they are up to. Press releases, product updates, whatever. This is the stuff they are proud of. Use it to your advantage.
- Look at the open jobs. Are there a lot of open roles or just this one? Are certain teams growing? Pocket this information away for your questions later.

Step 2: Move On To External Research

Glassdoor & Blind

Hot take: I don't read Glassdoor reviews before an interview. When was the last positive Glassdoor review you left for a company that you weren't asked to write? Glassdoor tends to skew negative, and it's silly to think any company doesn't have former employees with an axe to grind. Understand that there is a big difference between three out of five reviews being bad and that giving the company a 40% score on the one hand as opposed to hundreds of bad reviews reflecting a solid pattern of real problems. I try to get my own read on the company and then see whether Glassdoor confirms it or not, rather than going into the interview swayed by the opinions of people I don't know.

Layoff History
A quick Google search of "[Company] layoffs" tells you if they're expanding or struggling.

Funding & Acquisitions
Pages like Crunchbase show whether the company is growing aggressively or bracing for a downturn. Has it recently received funding? Is it publicly traded? How is it doing? You can also read news stories that the company didn't share on its website here.

Step 3: Hit up LinkedIn

- Check your interviewer's LinkedIn profile. Is there anything of interest to discuss with them?
- Look at the company's team page. Who are the key decision-makers? Who will be on your team? How big is the team?
- Search company and employee posts. Not finding much isn't a red flag, but you can find a lot of green flags by seeing how often employees talk about the company on LinkedIn.

Research Pitfalls to Avoid

Don't overdo it with the research. A few key insights are enough, especially for a first-round interview. This is why I recommend the ten-minute approach.
Don't ignore negative discoveries. These are great, big public red flags.
Don't memorize useless company facts without a good reason. I have seen so many candidates start reciting random facts, like the year we were founded, or what our last funding round was, with no real context for why they were

talking about those things. You're not writing a doctoral dissertation.

How to Use Research to Strengthen Your Interview Performance

You dug in, and you learned some of the things that really matter to the company. Now, it's time to use it to your advantage. Here's how to use your research strategically in your interview:

Tailor your answers using company insights. Instead of *"I love that your company values public service,"* say, *"I saw several employees posted about a community give-back day recently. I've participated in similar initiatives at X. How often does [company] have organized volunteer initiatives like this?"*

Ask questions that show you've done your homework. Instead of *"How's the company culture?"* ask, *"I noticed one of your company values is consistent two-way feedback, what are some successful ways you've seen employees give feedback to their managers?"* (I have a lot to say about asking good questions in an interview, like, a lot! Not to be all "like and follow for part 2", but more on this in Chapter 7, so keep reading!)

Position yourself as the solution. Instead of *"I have experience in digital marketing,"* say, *"I saw that you recently launched a new product in [category]. In my last role, I led digital campaigns for a similar launch and increased lead conversion by 30%. I'd love to bring that expertise to your team."*

SIDEBAR

Hey, it's me, Mike the realist, not Mike the guy giving you tips on how to get a job. Let's chat real quick because I know what you're thinking, and I hear it a lot, so I'll just address it now. I'm gonna swear a bunch for a second, if you don't like that, just jump back into reading the tips on how to get a job. That guy writing them is really smart!

"Why can't we all just be honest and stop these silly games?" Look, I could try to explain that it's not so much a game as companies trying to run a process that is inherently imperfect no matter how well it's done. But what I'll actually say is: Because that's f@$king life! You put up with this kind of bullshoot every day. We go through life putting on masks in lots of different situations. I don't want to have to wear pants to the grocery store, but I do because that's the norm there. The corporate world also has norms, and one of them is that we talk and act differently in that context than we do when we are with our friends. But guess what? You also get paid for it. So let's just accept that this is how it works, that it's not going to change anytime before you retire, and do the things that will help you get paid. Okay?

Hey, wait a second, I wrote curse words, what happened here? ARGH EDITOOOOORRRRSSSS!

The bottom line: Company research isn't about memorizing trivia. It's about understanding how the company operates, struggles, and grows so that you can position yourself as the ideal candidate. Do it right, and you won't just look prepared. You'll look like someone who already belongs on their team.

In the Interview: How to Answer Questions with Confidence and Be Memorable

Most of you don't remember this, but I will always remember my first-ever viral video, the one that set everything in motion for me and took me from about 5,000 to 30,000 followers on TikTok over one weekend. The video started, "I had five job interviews this week. I was asked five times, 'Tell me about yourself.' I was asked five times, 'Why do you want to work here?'" The point of the video was that job interviews are so much easier to prepare for than we realize. Sure, every now and then, you get thrown a curveball, but the truth is that most interviewers are never properly trained and ask the same questions that were asked of them by somebody who was asking the same questions asked of them. Interview questions are not only an opportunity for you to make a strong impression and make clear the value you bring to the company, they are a huge, impossible-to-miss ball right on the tee directly in front of you! (Please allow me this one sports analogy in this book.) I am amazed at how little prep work the average candidate does for an interview and how unprepared they are to answer questions they know they will be asked. Preparing to answer interview questions is not rocket science. It's really just first-grade math most of the time. You can't prepare for every possible question, but you can prepare to be sharp and impressive.

Build a Mental Question Framework

You can't control the outcome of a job interview. There are so many factors beyond your control, such as other candidates' performance, budgets, specific experience the company wants, etc. But look, if you head into a job interview and are not prepared for the common stuff, your failure is on you.

- There are zero excuses not to know your "tell me about yourself" elevator pitch. You don't need to read another blog post or watch another video about it. Trust me, I have about 30 of them. Stop overthinking it. Just prepare it.

- You have to be able to talk through your strengths and areas of opportunity.
- I can not help you if you are unprepared to answer, "Why do you want to work here?" even if we all know the real answer is "Cuz money!"

I'm going to talk way more about how to be ready to answer behavioral questions in the next few chapters, but this also feels like a great moment to pause and think through some very common interview questions. You have probably been asked all of these on a job interview before, and you're going to be asked all of them again. So my questions for you are: Do you have good answers to them? Did you practice the answers? Do you keep reworking the answers and fine-tuning? Or do you just wing it every time and act surprised you were asked the question and then wonder why the interview didn't go well?

Beyond "tell me about yourself," strengths and growth opportunities, and "why you want to work here," here are more questions you should always have prepared:

- Tell me about the hardest challenge you faced at a previous job.
- How do you handle tight deadlines?
- How do you handle having multiple priorities?
- Tell me about a mistake you made at work.
- Tell me about a time you had a conflict or disagreement with a coworker.

Beyond these, read the job description, especially the key responsibilities and requirements for this role, and start thinking through questions and scenarios that are likely to come up. Think of and quiz yourself about them. "What would you do if x?" when x are specific things you know could happen in this job. Think about when you've been in similar situations before. While we will talk more about behavioral interviews in the next chapter, refusing to prepare for them is asking not to do well.

Keep Your Brain in Shape

I've been there. I know how the job search can weigh on you. I especially know that if you're unemployed, brain fog can start to set in. But you need to stay sharp! Yes, you can prepare for a lot of common questions, but you also need to be able to think on your feet and pivot when the unexpected happens. I can not recommend enough that you do things like regularly solve brain teasers and thinking puzzles. Learn new complex things and try to explain them to your friends and family. Practice short (like one- to two-minute) impromptu speeches about random topics. This may sound silly, but your brain needs to be kept agile, and it needs practice. And while you are keeping your brain in shape, consider practicing answers to some less common questions, like personal insight questions such as, "What would your co-workers say about you?" or values-based questions like, "Do you hate to lose or love to win?" Something about appearing sharp and on top of things in an interview makes a candidate stand out, but you aren't going to just roll out of bed like that. Well, at least, I don't.

In the next chapter, I'm going to finally dive into the Core Four Stories for job interviewing (I know, I keep teasing stuff from upcoming chapters, but the reason I have broken job interviews up into so many chapters is because there is so much important stuff to say)! For now, I really want you to focus on the questions you get asked in an interview as your opportunity to shine and differentiate yourself from everyone else with your real, detailed, and impressive answers. For the most part, you are going to be asked the same questions over and over again, which means you can be ready for them. I know a lot of people think that everyone is so rehearsed in an interview and that interviewers hear the same answers over and over again, but as someone who has done thousands of them, I promise you that is not the case. I can tell who is underprepared, who is too scripted, and who is just making up a bunch of bull! It is worth taking the time to prepare well for interviews!

Respond to Curveballs with Confidence: The Pause-and-Pivot Method

The difference between candidates who handle curveball questions well and those who crumble isn't intelligence; it's preparation and mental framing. Here's how to master the pause-and-pivot technique:

The Pause

- Take three to five seconds to breathe deeply and organize your thoughts.
- Maintain confident body language, a slight smile, and shoulders back.
- Use bridging phrases like "That's an interesting question" or "Let me think about that for a moment."

The Pivot

- Reframe the question to highlight your strengths. "When you ask about unusual skills, I think about my ability to..."
- Connect your answer to relevant experience. "This reminds me of a situation where I..."
- Structuring your answer following the STAR method (situation, task, action, result) can be really helpful. I'm not someone who is going to force you to stick to a random acronym, but I do think it can help you formulate a strong, clear answer. I have a lot of thoughts on the STAR method, and I call my own addition to it the STAR+ method (clever, I know), which we will discuss in the next chapter.

Here are a bunch of questions I'm sure you'd rather not have to answer that you can apply the pause-and-pivot method to:

Scenario 1: The Odd Hypothetical
Interviewer: "How would you explain blockchain to a five-year-old?"
Candidate: [Pause] "That's a great question about communication skills. [Pivot] When explaining complex concepts, I find analogies work best. For a five-year-old, I'd say blockchain is like a magic diary that everyone can see, but only you can write on your own page using a special key. Once something is written down, nobody can erase it or change it without everyone noticing. I've used similar approaches when explaining technical concepts to our non-technical stakeholders, which helped us increase project buy-in by 40%."

Scenario 2: The Abstract Question
Interviewer: "If you were a type of tree, what would you be and why?"
Response: [Pause] "Interesting question about personal characteristics. [Pivot] I'd be an oak tree, adaptable to different environments, providing steady support for the ecosystem around me, and growing stronger over time. I've demonstrated these qualities in my work, particularly when I led my team through our company's acquisition, maintaining stability while adapting to new processes."

Scenario 3: The Impossible Scenario
Interviewer: "How would you determine the weight of a commercial airplane without using scales?"
Response: [Pause] "That's a great problem-solving challenge. [Pivot] I'd approach this by breaking it down into components we can estimate: looking up the manufacturer's specifications, calculating fuel weight based on distance traveled, and estimating passenger and cargo load. This methodical approach to complex problems is how I tackled our department's budget optimization. We had incomplete data but needed to make informed decisions."

Scenario 4: The Ethical Dilemma

Interviewer: "Tell me about a time you had to bend the rules to get something done."

Response: [Pause] "That's a thoughtful question about navigating constraints. [Pivot] While I believe in processes, I recognize when flexibility serves the greater good. When our client faced an emergency system outage, I bypassed the standard ticket queue, still documenting everything, to provide immediate assistance, then worked with our team afterward to improve our emergency protocols. This approach balanced immediate needs with long-term process integrity."

SIDEBAR

This is about the time in my TikTok comments where people start saying, "I wouldn't work for someone who asks dumb questions like that," and hey, that's your right. You can get up, tell them how your greatest weakness is that you can't stand dumb questions, march out of the office, and go brag to your friends. But this is real life, and you're reading a book about job searching, and we all know you aren't actually going to do that, and neither are the people who claim they will in their totally anonymous internet comments. Consider the questions as dumb as you like, but companies and managers are still going to ask them. Some of those companies are even really good places to work, and those managers may even be great managers. So once again, it is what it is. I can't fix everything you hate about the corporate world, but I can give you some strategies for dealing with this stuff to help you be more successful in it.

How to Recover If/When You Mess Up Mid-Interview

The pause-and-pivot method can help you navigate unexpected questions. But what about when you've already stumbled or made a mistake during the interview?
Even the best candidates can stumble. The key is knowing how to recover in real time.

If you ramble, stop yourself. "I realize I'm giving too much background. Let me jump to the key takeaway."
If you blank, buy time. "That's a great question. Let me think of the best example for that."
If you gave a weak answer, circle back later. "I'd love to revisit that earlier question. I have a stronger example."
If you get a question you weren't expecting, reframe it. "Are you looking for an example of x or y?"

Remember, everyone makes mistakes in interviews. It's how you handle them that sets you apart. Be prepared with these recovery techniques, and you'll show hiring managers you can think on your feet when the pressure's on, a skill that's way more valuable than a perfectly rehearsed answer.

Bring Ideas, Not Just Answers

Most candidates come prepared to answer questions. Outstanding candidates come prepared to contribute ideas. Bringing your ideas is not inherently presumptuous. Rather, it shows you've thought deeply about the role and the company. Here is a process for developing interview-ready ideas:

Research Phase
- Study the company's recent product launches, initiatives, or challenges.
- Review competitors' approaches and industry trends.
- Identify gaps or opportunities based on your expertise.

Idea Development
- Create one or two thoughtful suggestions or perspec-

tives related to the open role.

- Ensure your ideas are specific, actionable, and demonstrate your expertise.
- Prepare support for your ideas, but don't overwhelm them.

Presentation Approach

- Wait for an appropriate opening to naturally offer, "Based on what you've shared about x challenge..."
- Frame as a perspective, not a prescription, for example, "One approach that's worked in my experience..."
- Be open to feedback. "I'd love your thoughts on that approach."

Here's an example of what this might sound like in the real world: "I noticed from your recent product launch that you're moving from focusing only on enterprise-level clients to smaller commercial clients as well. In my previous role, we found that small businesses responded particularly well to implementation packages that included 30, 60, and 90-day milestone check-ins. Have you considered something like that?"

Being good at job interviews is a skill. You can call it a game if you want, but it's a skills-based one, not the game of pure chance you thought it was. Yes, you're going to spend time preparing for interviews for managers or jobs that ghost you. Yes, you'll bring ideas to an interview for a job you don't have yet. But just like every other skill, you get better at it with practice. Instead of DMing me to say it's dumb that the job goes to the best interviewer, let's just work on helping you become the best interviewer!

A Real World Success Story

The following is a real DM (slightly edited for privacy) that I received so close to publishing this book that I had to go back into the final draft and delete someone else's story because I liked this one more. Sorry to the person whose story I deleted. You'll never know!

Hi Mike. I know you've said that you can't keep up with your DMs, so even if you never read this, I still want to send all of my gratitude and praise your way for all of the time you spend making videos about interviewing and applying for jobs. I have been following you for the past year and slowly understanding, adopting, and absorbing your content, and it became so simple in my head that I finally had a third-round interview for my dream job today, and I just received an offer tonight—just hours after the interview!! I have never subscribed to following anyone before, but I was always excited to see your new videos. Your honesty, vulnerability, and realistic advice is the only time I've ever seen a person on social media genuinely just want to help people for maybe nothing in return. After a terrible interview experience that set me back entirely from wanting to try anymore at all and broke me (my interviewers told me 15 minutes into the interview that I seemed like someone who "would need too much handholding" and "they didn't have time for that"), I finally got another interview, and every round was exactly how you always said it would go so that when I got to my final interview, I was laughing before every question because I already had the exact answer and wasn't afraid of their questions. It literally felt like you were right there cheering me on the whole time.

Mike's take: Here's the thing about this DM—and trust me, I deleted a lot of the stuff talking about how good I am to just focus on the interview—I didn't do anything for this person other than point them in the same direction I'm pointing you. I can't make every interview go well. I can't promise you a job, but this person got better at interviewing just by doing the things that work.

Red Flags or Annoyances: What Actually Matters in an Interview Process

Most job seekers walk into an interview hyper-alert for anything that *feels off*. A hiring manager stumbles over an answer? A recruiter reschedules? Clearly, this company is doomed. But let's be real: not every weird moment in an interview is a red flag, and not every red flag is a dealbreaker.

Hiring processes are imperfect. Companies are run by humans, and humans make mistakes (= are human). The key is knowing which of those mistakes are minor hiccups—and which ones are screaming alarms telling you to run for the hills. Here's the part most job seekers forget: You are also in control. You are not at their mercy. The hiring process is just as much about you vetting them as it is about them vetting you. If you see red flags that make you hesitate, trust your gut. Things rarely get better than the impression they initially make on you.

Type	Example	What It Likely Means	How to Handle It
Annoyance	The interviewer was five minutes late.	They're busy. Not ideal, but not a red flag.	A simple, "No problem. I understand schedules can be tight" shows grace. You're probably late to things too now and again.
Red Flag	The interviewer had no idea who you were or why you were there.	Poor internal communication could signal larger structural issues.	Ask directly: "It seems there might have been a communication gap. How does the team typically handle project handoffs?"
Annoyance	The recruiter had to reschedule once or twice.	Schedules shift. Life happens.	Be flexible: "Happy to accommodate. Would Tuesday at 2 p.m. work instead?" Think about how many meetings you've probably moved.

Type	Example	What It Likely Means	How to Handle It
Red Flag	The recruiter ghosted you after multiple rounds.	This company doesn't respect candidates' time.	After your second follow-up email goes unanswered, it's time to focus on other opportunities.
Annoyance	The interviewer asked a cliche or bad interview question.	They may not be a great interviewer, but that doesn't mean they aren't a good manager.	Take a breath, structure your thoughts, and tackle it methodically. We prepare for these questions because we get asked these questions.
Red Flag	The interviewer was rude, dismissive, or aggressive.	This is not going well, and you don't want to work for this person.	Trust your gut. Consider asking, "I noticed the conversation feels tense. Is this still an okay time for us to have the conversation?"

What's Just Annoying?

As I've said, not every annoyance is a red flag. A trait among job seekers that I have noticed in the last few years is that they are looking for any reason to hate a company, and trust me, I get it. But we don't have to try so hard to find molehills to make mountains out of when some of these companies have plenty of real, big ol' mountains already. These, for example, are some things that are simply annoying that you should be willing to overlook during an interview process:

Slow response times. Hiring isn't always a company's top priority. Internal delays happen. Give them grace if communication is otherwise professional.
Awkward small talk. Not every interviewer is outgoing or a great communicator, that doesn't mean they are bad to work for. Judge them on substantive exchanges, not whether they were smooth, and ask about your weekend.
A few tough or bad questions. Just because they asked a question you weren't expecting, or a lame cliche question

like "What's your greatest weakness?" doesn't mean they were trying to trick you or that the job isn't good. Most managers, even the really good ones, have never been trained to conduct great interviews.

A disorganized panel interview. Large teams mean multiple opinions. One unstructured interview doesn't mean the company is a disaster. Look at how the people interviewing you interacted with each other. Do they respect each other's questions and time?

Technical Difficulties: Zoom crashes, microphones fail, and meeting rooms get double-booked. How they handle these hiccups can tell you more than the problems themselves.

None of these should be a dealbreaker. They are just a part of life. If we all refused to work for every awkward or untrained manager, none of us would ever have a job. Stop focusing on these ticky-tacky things and look for actual red flags.

Red Flags, Big and Small

Red flags aren't always obvious, like a screaming boss or an office that looks like a scene from *The Office*. Often, red flags are more subtle signals that reveal deeper issues. The reason I say to stop focusing on little things like an interview that wasn't organized or a slow process is that those are the kinds of things that happen everywhere. Pobody is nerfect, and when we focus on stuff like feedback not being quick before the next round, we tend to miss the things that actually reveal themselves as red flags during the interview. Here are some examples of more subtle red flags:

Vague answers to specific questions. When you ask about turnover and they respond with platitudes about "fit" or "high standards" without specific numbers or causes, they're hiding something.

Inconsistent information. Different interviewers giving conflicting details about the role, reporting structure, or expectations suggests internal confusion or deliberate misdirection.

Dismissive treatment of your questions. When interviewers seem annoyed by thoughtful questions, it reveals a culture that doesn't value curiosity or employee input.

Overpromising. If everything sounds too perfect or they're making extraordinary promises about growth, autonomy, or advancement without specifics, they're likely selling you their dream scenario. They may not be intentionally misleading, but they're probably only focusing on how they would love it to be.

And then there are the brighter-than-the-sun, bigger-than-the-flags-they-fly-at-midwestern-car-dealerships, big ol' red flags:

High turnover. If they're always hiring for the same role, ask why. *"I noticed this position has been posted several times this year. Are they each new growth positions?"* If the answer is vague or defensive, proceed with caution.

Dodging questions about culture. If they sidestep questions about work-life balance or company values, there's a reason. **Press gently.** *"Could you share a specific example of how the team balances tight deadlines with personal time?"* If they can't give concrete examples, that tells you something.

Bad-mouthing employees. If an interviewer complains about former (or worse, current) employees, assume you'll be the next one they talk about. Listen for phrases like "people just don't want to work hard" or "the last person couldn't handle the pressure." These are huge flashing warning signs.

Unclear reporting structure. If multiple people give different answers about who you'd report to, expect chaos. Try, *"I've heard different perspectives on the reporting structure. Could you clarify how decisions are typically made on the team?"* If they can't align on basics, imagine working there daily.

Mismatched values in action. Watch how they treat you

during the interview process. Are they respectful of your time? Do they follow through on commitments? A company that says it values respect but keeps you waiting 30 minutes is showing its true colors.

Of course, not all red flags are created equal, and a deal-breaker for me may not be a deal-breaker for you (and vice versa). So while it's good to have a general idea of what real red flags are, big and small, it's more important to understand which red flags you can look past and which you can't. There is no perfect job, so if you're going to run from every little hiccup, you're going to be looking for a long time. BIG BUT (hehe), when your gut is screaming to run, it's probably right. Are multiple red flags showing up every round? Are your direct questions consistently being deflected? Or worse yet, is the manager becoming defensive of your reasonable questions? Are there clear signs that this job is going to be a nightmare? People generally show you their best at a job interview; things don't usually get better from there. I have had plenty of job opportunities where I eventually decided it was best to cut bait and run. In the moment, it may feel wrong because you need a job, but you'll thank yourself eventually.

Tactical Dialogue Examples: How to Address Red Flags in Real Time

Sure, there may be some red flags that make you recognize right away as signs (red flags!) that you need to get as far away from this company as possible. If an interviewer is berating you, or saying awful things about a group of people, or co-workers, you can probably assume it's safe to just finish up the interview and move on to the next opportunity. But in other cases, a lot of things that appear to be red flags may simply be poor communication about something or an issue that can be worked through. Just as you want a company to understand that you have flaws but still hire you for your strengths, the same can be said about a job.

If you are trying to figure out whether something is an annoyance or a red flag, big or small, the best thing you can do is dig a bit deeper to see what's beneath the surface. Perhaps the interview was positive, but the hiring manager gave one response about late-night work on a recent project. Instead of assuming that everyone works late nights all the time, ask a follow-up question like, "What do you think caused that project to have to be finished up off hours?" or "How often do scenarios like that arise?" Such questions may reveal that this was the first time it ever happened and that the manager gave everyone a half day to make up for it. I focus so much on asking good questions and letting them come from the interview itself because these are the opportunities to learn more, dig a bit deeper, and get as clear a picture of the environment as you can.

Here are some examples of ways to turn questionable responses into a deeper conversation with strategic follow-up questions.

Scenario 1: Vague Answer About Turnover
Interviewer: "We have high standards, so not everyone is a good fit long-term."
Weak Response: "Oh, I see. That makes sense."
Strong Response: "I appreciate maintaining standards. What specific qualities have separated successful team members from those who've moved on? I want to make sure I understand what success looks like here."

Scenario 2: Unclear Expectations
Interviewer: "The role is fluid and will evolve based on business needs."
Weak Response: "I'm flexible and ready for anything!"
Strong Response: "I thrive in evolving environments. To better understand, could you walk me through how the priorities for this role have shifted over the past year? And what core responsibilities have remained consistent?"

Scenario 3: Work-Life Balance Concerns
Interviewer: "We work hard here. Sometimes that means putting in extra hours to get things done."
Weak Response: "No problem, I'm used to working long

hours."

Strong Response: "I'm certainly committed to delivering results. How does the team typically handle high-demand periods? Are there specific systems or approaches to help maintain sustainability during intense project phases?"

Mike's Snarky Do's and Don'ts for Job Interviews

DO research companies like a first date you met on Bumble, not like your report is due on Monday. Companies don't care if you know their founding date. They care if you understand their problems.

DO ask targeted questions that showcase your research. "I noticed you recently expanded into [x-market]. How is that affecting your team's priorities?" beats "What's your company culture like?" every time.

DO trust your gut when you see red flags. Unless you think everything is a red flag!

DO take three to five seconds to breathe and think before answering tough questions. That thoughtful pause makes you look confident, not clueless.

DO craft signature stories that showcase your unique approach and measurable results. Vague claims about being "detail-oriented" put hiring managers to sleep.

DON'T treat minor interview hiccups like apocalyptic red flags. A rescheduled meeting isn't the same as being ghosted after three rounds of interviews.

DON'T panic when asked unexpected questions. "How would you explain blockchain to a five-year-old?" is testing your communication skills, not your blockchain expertise.

DON'T give generic answers when specific ones will make you memorable. "I increased conversion by 30%" beats "I'm good at marketing" every.single.time.

DON'T mistake tough interview questions for trick questions. Most of the time, they're genuinely trying to see how you think, not trying to trap you.

DON'T accept vague answers about high turnover, unclear expectations, or a toxic work culture. If they can't give straight answers in the interview, imagine working there daily.

CHAPTER SIX

Mastering Behavioral Interviews

TL;DR

If you can't effectively communicate how you think, handle challenges, and deliver results, you will struggle to get hired. It's that simple. Behavioral interviews separate those who merely look good on paper from those who truly deliver in real-world situations. This chapter teaches you how to master behavioral interviews: how to structure impactful responses, focus on your four core stories, and avoid common pitfalls that cost candidates the opportunity every day.

Most people view behavioral interviews as a painful hoop to jump through. They rehearse a few robotic STAR responses, recycle the same old stories, and wonder why their interviews fall flat. But simply having a polished story about "working well on a team" isn't enough. Interviewers aren't interested in nice stories. They want clear, compelling proof that you can think on your feet, solve tough problems, and deliver results that matter.

If you're tired of leaving interviews feeling uncertain or wondering why you weren't chosen, it's time to upgrade your approach. In this chapter, you'll learn why hiring managers rely on behavioral interviews, how they evaluate your answers, and why relying solely on the STAR method isn't going to cut it. Behavioral interviews aren't just a formality—they're literally the difference between "Thanks, but no thanks" and an actual paycheck. No pressure or anything.

(Oh, and before this chapter starts, remember that sidebar in the previous chapter about how this is just how it is and complaining about games and all that other junk won't help? That goes triple for this chapter.)

Why Behavioral Interviews Matter and How to Crush Them

Behavioral interviews aren't some random or arbitrary hiring practice. They're an essential strategy companies use to make hiring decisions fairer, smarter, and more predictive. If you've ever wondered why you're constantly asked to *"Tell a story about a time when..."* it's because companies need concrete evidence of your skills, not just vague assurances that you're good at your job. Imagine two candidates: Both claim they're fantastic problem-solvers, and both have similar experience and credentials listed on their resumes. How does a hiring manager choose between them? Behavioral questions level the playing field by forcing candidates to demonstrate their skills by giving real-life examples. It's not enough to say "I'm a great leader," you need to show exactly how you've led a team through a tough project or navigated tricky workplace conflicts. Everyone is judged against the same clear, consistent criteria.

Think about hiring for a customer service role. One candidate says, "I'm great with difficult customers." Another candidate shares a story about calmly resolving a complicated customer issue that not only retained the client but also improved the company's overall customer satisfaction rating by 10%. Which candidate would you choose? Exactly. You would offer the job to the candidate who demonstrated their impact with specific examples.

Behavioral interviews also help hiring managers cut through bias and gut feelings. Sure, charisma and confidence matter, but they're not enough. Behavioral questions force interviewers to evaluate actual accomplishments, not just personality or how well someone matches the vague ideal candidate they are imagining.

Behavioral interviews also dramatically reduce the likelihood of making a hiring mistake. Consider the alternative—companies relying on gut instincts, vibes, or vague impressions. That's risky because someone can interview brilliantly yet fail on the job. Instead, structured behavioral questions require candidates to show how they approached past challenges. If you've successfully managed tough deadlines before, there's a good chance you'll handle them well in the future. Conversely, candidates who stumble when asked for specifics often reveal a gap between their claims and their abilities.

Past behavior is the strongest predictor of future performance. When you're asked about how you've previously solved problems, managed teams, or handled failures, it's not because hiring managers enjoy making you squirm. Your detailed responses allow them to envision how you might perform within their company. Did you adapt to challenges, find creative solutions, or simply muddle through? Your stories give hiring managers a clear preview of what to expect if they bring you on board.

Another underrated benefit of behavioral interviews is practicality. Hiring managers and recruiters deal with high volumes of applicants, many of whom have similar backgrounds. Behavioral questions efficiently separate those who can demonstrate clear results from those who can't. Instead of wasting time on theoretical discussions, behavioral questions cut straight to real-world skills. This helps streamline the hiring process, saving companies time and resources while ensuring they choose the candidate best equipped to succeed.

In short, behavioral interviews aren't going anywhere. They're sticking around because they work. They level the playing field, reduce bias, and significantly boost a company's ability to predict your success. For you, the candidate, mastering behavioral interviews is your best chance to prove you have what it takes to excel in the role. By structuring your answers effectively, showcasing real impact, and demonstrating clear thought processes, you transform from just another applicant into the clear choice for the job. Understanding this puts you miles ahead of candidates who treat behavioral interviews as a mere formality or, worse, an annoyance. Remember, you're not just telling stories—you're providing proof. You're not just saying you can do the job; you're demonstrating exactly why hiring you is the smartest decision they could make.

Most job seekers walk into a behavioral interview thinking, I just need to tell a good story. They rehearse a few generic STAR (situation, task, action, result) method answers, feel good about their delivery, and then wonder why they didn't make it past the second round. The problem? Hiring managers don't just want a story. They want proof that you can solve problems, think critically, and deliver results. That's why behavioral interviews exist in the first place.

How Candidates Are Actually Evaluated in Behavioral Interviews

Most candidates assume that if they *answer the question*, they've done enough. Wrong. Hiring managers don't just want you to describe a situation. They want to see how you think, how you problem-solve, and how much impact you actually had.

Evaluation Criteria	What It Means
Relevance to the Role	Does your answer actually demonstrate a skill they care about?
Depth of Response	Are you just listing what happened? Or are you explaining how you tackled the problem?
Measurable Impact	Did you actually make a difference? Or were you just completing assigned tasks?
Clear, Logical Thinking	Can you explain your thought process in a way that makes sense?

Do you want to know the biggest mistake candidates make? They spend too much time describing the "situation" and not enough on the "action." The best answers don't just say what happened—they show the bigger impact of your actions.

A Real World Success Story

Consider Sarah, a seasoned software engineer who consistently advanced to initial interview rounds but rarely secured a job offer. Frustrated, Sarah sought guidance and realized the weakness was not her skills or experience—it was how she communicated her stories during behavioral interviews.

Initially, Sarah answered behavioral questions by merely listing tasks or responsibilities she had in previous roles. For instance, when asked, *"Tell me about a significant challenge you overcame,"* she typically responded with something like, "At my last job, I handled software bugs and maintained our database systems. We fixed issues and kept things running smoothly." Her responses were technically correct, but they lacked clarity, depth, and measurable impact, making her seem just like every other candidate.

Realizing the need for improvement, Sarah shifted her approach and adopted the STAR+ method. She focused not only on the tasks she performed but on clearly articulating the impact of her actions. She transformed her responses into results-oriented narratives, making them concise, engaging, and memorable.

When she was next asked about overcoming a challenge, Sarah answered, "At my previous role, our core product had stability issues, which caused customer frustration and increased service tickets. I recognized the urgency, and I took the lead to analyze the root causes of the recurring bugs, developed a targeted debugging plan, and collaborated closely with our customer success team to prioritize fixes based on customer impact. Within two months, we reduced system downtime by 45%, slashed customer complaints by 30%, and increased our customer retention rate significantly. This not only improved our customer satisfaction scores but directly contributed to a noticeable uptick in renewals, ultimately boosting company revenue."

Sarah's refined answers provided exactly what hiring managers were looking for: proof of critical thinking, clear initiative, and tangible results. By shifting her storytelling from generic tasks to clear, measurable impacts, Sarah immediately stood out from other candidates. This change dramatically improved her interview performance, leading to multiple final-round interviews and ultimately securing her a senior engineering role at a prestigious tech company.

Sarah's transformation illustrates exactly why mastering impact-driven narratives is essential. Hiring managers don't just want to hear what you did. They need you to spell out why it mattered.

**HEY READER...YEA YOU...
DON'T SKIP THIS NEXT PART, OKAY?**

The Core Four Stories: The Best Interview Tip You'll Get

If you've followed me for a while, you've heard me talk about the Core Four Stories ad nauseam. One reason I do that is because it goes viral every time, and this guy loves that TikTok creator fund money! The other reason I talk about the Core Four a lot is that it's really f%$@ing good advice! I have gotten more comments and messages about this advice helping people land jobs than any other advice I give. It's battle-tested and will make interviewing a lot easier for you. The first time I ever sold a digital product was an e-book that contained all of the info I'm about to give you here!

Most behavioral interview questions fall into a few predictable categories. By having four key, well-structured stories prepared, you can confidently respond to nearly any behavioral question. When prepared correctly, these stories are flexible enough to adapt to different interview scenarios, allowing you to demonstrate your skills, experiences, and impact clearly. Knowing these stories will reduce your stress level, make you a more memorable candidate, and show that you prepared. You'll never have to panic about finding an answer to a question. These stories will help you stand out from the other candidates. And you'll feel more confident and ready.

You don't need countless anecdotes, just four strong, versatile narratives:

1. Your Most Successful Project: Think back to a project where you excelled and achieved great results. Can you explain the context, the challenges, and your role in the success of the project?
Some questions you will be able to answer in an interview by knowing this story include:

- Tell me about a time you demonstrated leadership skills. This is a great opportunity for people who want more leadership responsibilities in their next role but have not officially had them in a previous role.
- Describe a situation where you had to manage multiple priorities or a tight deadline.
- Share a situation where you had to adapt and overcome an unexpected challenge.
- Tell me about a time you took initiative to drive an important change.
- Tell me about a time you worked well with a team.

2. Your Least Successful Project: Believe it or not, being asked about failures in a job interview is not a trick. These questions are not traps to see if you admit to being imperfect. But don't pretend you're perfect! Interviewers appreciate candidates who can handle adversity and learn from their mistakes, which makes really understanding how to tell this story a valuable opportunity to show both your resilience and adaptability.

- Some questions you will be able to answer in an interview by knowing this story include:
- Tell me about how you handle setbacks during work.
- Tell me about a time you had to pivot due to a setback.
- Tell me about a situation where you had to take responsibility for a mistake.
- Tell me about a time you realized your project was not on track to meet goals and what you did from there.
- Describe a project you worked on that had conflicting priorities or unclear objectives.

3. Your Most Difficult Stakeholders: Working with challenging stakeholders is common in many roles. You need to be able to describe an experience where you successfully managed a difficult relationship, possibly even several, depending on your role. Demonstrating your interpersonal skills and conflict resolution abilities will leave a positive impression on interviewers and show a high level of emotional intelligence. The key is not whether you were right or wrong or won or lost. The key is how you solved the problem as professionally as possible.

- Some questions you will be able to answer in an interview by knowing this story include:
- Can you share a time you received significant pushback on your work from a key stakeholder?
- Share a situation where you had to communicate difficult or sensitive information to a stakeholder. How did you prepare for the conversation? And how did you ensure the message was conveyed effectively?
- Can you recall a time when you had to deal with a stakeholder who was uncooperative or resistant to change? How did you gain their trust and buy-in for the proposed changes?
- Tell me about a time you disagreed with a stakeholder who was more senior than you but you still knew you were correct.

4. Your Passion Project: This story is your chance to showcase your enthusiasm for anything work-related. Managers love this, no matter how much it makes you cringe.
Some questions you will be able to answer in an interview by knowing this story:

- What is the ideal next role for you? What would you be working on?
- What are you most proud of so far in your career?

- What do you find most rewarding about your job?
- Can you share a specific instance where you found great satisfaction in completing a task or project?

The Versatility of the Core Four

I'm often asked if you can tell the same story again, and the answer is yes, but you have to branch off from it a bit. Perhaps, you tell a story about making a big sale when asked about your most successful project. You may later be asked about how you worked well with a team, and you can reference the big sale story you've already told, but now it's time to discuss the teamwork that went into it. (This also saves you the time and trouble of setting the situation up again.) Or you may have already told this story, but now you are being asked about a challenge you overcame, so you can point to the story you told earlier, but dig in deeper to a challenge that came up in the sales process that you didn't include when you told the overall story the first time.

Think of these four stories like giant tree branches, each branch with several branches of offshoots. Your story is the branch, but all the smaller branches are details of the story you don't tell every time because there are far too many for one story. You can adjust where you go and what you include each time you tell the story based on the questions you are asked. But in order to be able to do that, you first have to prepare them and know them really well!

Most job seekers don't bomb behavioral interviews because they lack experience—they fail because they give weak, rambling, or forgettable answers. They overexplain irrelevant details, undersell their results, or worse, sound like they're reading a script. Being a good interviewer means also being a good storyteller, and luckily, that's a skill you can practice and learn. Or you can just do what some of you may be doing and shake your head and say "BUT I SHOULDN'T HAAAAAVVVEEE TOOOO!!!!" And that's fine too. Remember, I'm just trying to help you get a job.

SIDEBAR

Hey, let's chat for a sec. You're probably sick of having the STAR method shoved in your face, right? So here's the thing, STAR is not a rule. You'll hear people talk about it like it's a rule, but they don't know what they're saying. The STAR method is really just a way to make sure you tell a story efficiently. You don't have to tell a story by saying: here is the situation, here is the task, here is the action, here is the result. These are just the necessary elements of a good story. You will hear people call it the BAR (Behavior, Action, Results), the CAR (Context, Action, Results), the CARL (Context, Action, Results, Learnings), etc. It's all the same thing!

I like sticking with STAR when I talk through this stuff because it's most common, but don't get stuck in making sure you are going S…T…A…R every time you tell a story, just learn to tell a good story. My publishers told me I should create my own acronym, and after a few funny ChatGPT results, I told them I don't want to because the acronym isn't that important. We went back and forth and settled on just adding a + for some of that "Mike twist." Stop worrying about what it's called, though, and just take these notes on how to tell good stories and get the job, okay? Great! See you back in the book.

The STAR+ Method

STAR—situation, task, action, result—is a solid starting point, but most candidates treat it like a rigid checklist rather than an effective storytelling framework. When misused, STAR leads to predictable, robotic responses that blend into the background noise of every other candidate.

Here's the reality check: Hiring managers mentally check out when you start overexplaining your story. Seriously, they're not looking for your autobiography. Most interviewees overload their responses with unnecessary context (the situation and task), leaving interviewers bored, long before the candidate reaches the good stuff. Worse still, because they spent so long talking about the situation and task, they feel rushed by the end, sense the boredom from interviewers, and often rush through the result, the primary opportunity to demonstrate their impact. Saying "and then we fixed it" does nothing to demonstrate actual impact—it's forgettable and weak.

Common STAR Mistakes and How to Fix Them

Mistake	Why It Fails	How to Fix It
Too much setup	The hiring manager tunes out before you get to the good part.	Keep the situation & task under 20% of your response.
Too vague on actions	Just saying *"I helped the team solve a problem"* isn't compelling.	Highlight your specific contributions. What did you do?
Weak or missing results	*"We completed the project."* Cool. But did it matter?	Show impact: *"We cut project time by 30% and saved $50,000."*
Forgetting to connect to the job	A great story that doesn't prove you're right for this role is a wasted answer.	End with: "This experience strengthened my ability to [KEY SKILL], which is why I'd excel in this role."

How to Elevate Your Behavioral Interview: The STAR+ Method

To truly set yourself apart, upgrade from basic STAR responses with what I call the STAR+ Method, your impact amplifier:

Situation: Keep it concise, no more than two sentences. Briefly set the context, highlighting only what's absolutely essential to understand your story.
Task: Clearly outline the specific challenge or goal. Frame it as meaningful, high-stakes, and genuinely worth solving.
Action: Here's where you shine. Clearly articulate your unique contributions. What did you specifically do that

made a difference? Highlight your thought process and why you chose that particular approach.
Result: Quantify your achievements. Instead of vague statements like, "It was successful," say something tangible: "We improved efficiency by 20%" or "We cut down time from three days to one."
+ (Tie it to the Role): Finish by explicitly linking your experience to the position you're interviewing for. For example, "This experience strengthened my ability to manage complex projects under pressure, aligning directly with your team's current initiatives."

How to Quantify Impact, Even Without Hard Numbers

Not every job provides detailed metrics. That doesn't mean you can't quantify impact. You can say things like, "I introduced a new process that reduced errors significantly, saving considerable time," "My approach led to a noticeable improvement in customer satisfaction, with positive feedback increasing considerably," and "Compared to previous methods, my strategy increased efficiency substantially."

Here are some other methods for quantifying impact without hard numbers:

Use estimates. "Improved efficiency by approximately 20%."
Make comparative statements. "The new approach was significantly faster than previous processes."
Articulate qualitative improvements. Clearly outline meaningful improvements like increased morale, enhanced collaboration, or reduced conflict.
Align with business goals. Connect your actions to broader organizational achievements or priorities.

A Real World Case Study

Jessica, a project manager, previously focused her interview responses on generic descriptions: "I ensured projects were delivered on time." Realizing this was too vague, she focused on the Core Four Stories she kept hearing me talk about. She prepped these stories, wrote outlines for them, and filled in all of the details for herself. Once she got into the interview, she felt confident and could only help but laugh as she was asked all the standard behavioral questions. Only this time she had a real success story to tell, "The software project had fallen behind schedule, but I was able to eliminate this redundant task to help the team catch back up and deliver it not only on time, but under budget."

Using this results-driven approach, and ensuring she knew her Core Four Stories, Jessica effectively addressed multiple interview questions about improving processes, managing challenging clients, and recovering from mistakes, ultimately securing a higher-level role with a substantial salary increase.

Using STAR doesn't mean checking off boxes—it means telling a strong, results-driven story that proves you're the best fit for the job. If you use the STAR+ method to highlight impact, amplify results, and connect your answer back to the role, you won't just answer interview questions—you'll stand out from every other candidate. Hiring managers don't just want to hear what you did. They want to see why it mattered.

Behavioral Questions in Technical Interviews: Why They Matter and How to Excel

If you're interviewing for a technical role, you might think your coding skills, algorithm mastery, or data expertise alone will land you the job. Think again. Technical skills matter, but companies don't hire just for technical prowess—they hire people who can communicate clearly, collaborate effectively, and handle real-world pressures. The behavioral portion of a technical interview isn't an afterthought; it's often what separates great candidates from average ones.

Why Behavioral Interviews Are Essential for Technical Roles

Technical roles aren't just about coding, building models, or solving algorithms. Employers use behavioral questions to ensure you're not just technically competent but practically effective in real-world scenarios. They want to know about the following:

Critical Thinking: Can you clearly explain your thought process, not just your solution?
Adaptability: How do you handle unexpected setbacks, tight deadlines, or challenges?
Collaboration: Can you effectively work within teams, or are you someone who struggles to connect with others?
Decision-Making: When faced with tradeoffs or competing technical approaches, how do you prioritize and make decisions?

Common Behavioral Questions for Technical Interviews

Understanding why employers ask these questions helps you prepare better answers, and better yet, you can use your Core Four Stories to answer all of these questions!

Question Type	Why It Matters	Example Questions
Problem-Solving	Tests your ability to handle complexity and adapt under pressure.	"Tell me about a time you had to debug a critical technical issue."
Collaboration & Teamwork	Measures your ability to work effectively with others.	"Describe a situation where you disagreed with a team member. How did you resolve it?"
Handling Pressure & Failure	Assesses resilience and adaptability when things go wrong.	"Tell me about a project you worked on that failed. What did you learn?"
Decision-Making & Tradeoffs	Evaluates your analytical approach and decision-making capability.	"Describe a time you chose between two competing solutions. What influenced your decision?"

Structuring Effective Answers: The STAR+ Method

Behavioral answers in technical interviews require clarity, precision, and a focus on outcomes. Use STAR+ to structure your responses:

Situation: Set up the technical scenario briefly.
Task: Clearly define your responsibility.
Action: Detail your approach, highlighting your unique contributions, considerations, and trade-offs.
Result: Clearly state measurable outcomes: improvements in efficiency, performance, or team success.
+ Tie it to the Role: Explicitly connect the outcome to the skills required by the job you're interviewing for.

Common Mistakes Technical Candidates Make and How to Avoid Them

Mistake	Why It Fails	How to Fix It
Focusing only on technical details	Interviewers need to see the business impact of your work.	Connect technical accomplishments directly to measurable outcomes, e.g., "My optimization reduced load time by 25%."
Neglecting the decision-making process	Your approach matters as much as your solution.	Explain why you chose your approach and the alternatives you considered.
Ignoring collaboration aspects	Technical roles still require teamwork and communication.	Highlight interactions and collaborative efforts explicitly, e.g., "I coordinated closely with the design team to integrate feedback quickly."
Not linking back to the role	Stories without relevance waste opportunities to demonstrate fit.	Always end with relevance: "This experience directly built my expertise in X, a key component of this role."

A Real World Case Study: Behavioral Questions Transforming Technical Interviews

Initially, Jake, a talented data scientist, believed excelling at technical tests alone would land him roles at major tech companies. Despite acing technical assessments, he consistently failed final rounds of interviews because his behavioral answers lacked depth and clarity. Realizing this, he adjusted his approach to behavioral responses. Instead of simply describing technical solutions, Jake began explicitly outlining his thought process, including why he chose particular methods, the trade-offs he considered, and the measurable impacts of his decisions. For example, he turned an initially bland debugging story into a compelling narrative: "Facing persistent performance issues, I methodically isolated bottlenecks, implemented targeted code improvements, and reduced system latency by 40%, significantly enhancing user experience and customer satisfaction scores." This shift dramatically improved interview feedback, eventually landing him a position at a top-tier tech company.

Behavioral questions in technical interviews aren't just about storytelling. They're about showcasing that you're not just skilled technically but also capable of delivering impactful, real-world results.

MIKE'S SNARKY DO'S AND DON'TS OF BEHAVIORAL INTERVIEWS

DO prepare your Core Four Stories. Seriously, if you're not going to prep, just put my book down. I'm not for you!

DO always focus on impact. What changed because of your work? Vague claims mean nothing.

DO keep it concise. Please stop rambling. Prepare, answer the question, and stop talking!

DO link everything directly back to the role. Don't make interviewers guess why your story matters.

DO practice, but stay human. They're hiring a person, not a script.

DON'T spend all day setting up your story. Cut to the action and impact quickly.

DON'T give away the credit by constantly saying "we." Own your story. What did YOU do?

DON'T assume technical brilliance alone will save you. Being good at your job isn't enough if you can't clearly articulate why your work matters.

Behavioral interviews aren't optional. They're your chance to prove your worth clearly. Master these techniques, and you'll go from just another applicant to the candidate hiring managers can't afford not to hire.

Before We Begin

In this chapter, I'm going to discuss a lot of similar-sounding questions. I'm going to call some questions bad or good, but the truth is that almost any question can be a good one in a particular situation.

The most important thing to keep in mind when we talk about interview questions is that the best questions come from a place of genuine curiosity and are based on the conversation you've been having so far. I want to highlight that early because whenever I talk about interview questions, people inevitably tell me that interviews should be a conversation and not some scripted play. I agree! The questions I suggest are not a script. They are not a rule, and you do not have to ask them. They are suggestions and ideas meant to get you thinking more deeply about the questions you ask.

Most good interview questions start with phrases like "you mentioned" or "earlier you said," making it clear that they are based on your actual conversation, not something you wrote down and ask every single person you interview with. Please do not treat this chapter like a script to write out for yourself. Think of it as a guideline.

Why Strong Candidates Ask Smart Questions

Imagine you're on a first date, and the other person sits back, answers your questions politely but never asks a single thing about you. At some point, you'll start thinking, *Do they even care? Do they want to get to know me? Do they think I'm pretty?* That's how hiring managers feel when candidates fail to ask smart, engaging questions during an interview.

Do you remember a couple of chapters ago when I told you to stop being scared of losing the job and start trying to get it? WELL, THIS IS YOUR CHANCE TO DO THAT. I literally screamed that in my head when I wrote it, so please hear me yelling.

Most people view job interviews as a test, as a one-way interrogation in which the company holds all the power, and the candidate just has to endure it and hope they land the job. But here's the truth: Strong candidates know that interviews aren't just about proving they can do the job. They know that interviews are also about making sure they want to do the job. The ability to ask thoughtful questions separates the desperate from the discerning, the forgettable from the memorable, and, in many cases, the rejected from the hired.

But why, Mike? I'm so glad you asked! Simply put, the time you get in an interview to ask questions is the one time when you have complete control. Up until this point, you have been responding, defending, and boasting, and the ball has been in the interviewer's court. But now, at this moment, the ball is in your court. It is your turn. You get to ask *whatever* you want! Sure, you probably shouldn't ask *whatever* you want, but you still could.

When you shift your mindset from "I hope they like me" to "Let's see if this is a place I'd actually want to work," the whole game changes. The way you ask questions signals confidence, intelligence, and strategic thinking, qualities hiring managers actively look for. Many candidates completely miss this opportunity. They either don't ask anything (screaming, "I just want a paycheck"), or they ask the same boring questions that every other applicant throws out there. But who do hiring managers actually notice? The people who ask good questions. They stand out. They are more engaged, more prepared, and frankly, more hireable.

Your questions shape the interviewer's perception of you. Your resume gets you in the door, but your ability to hold a strong conversation determines whether you get the offer. If you don't ask anything, the interviewer assumes you're just another person looking for any job rather than this job. If you ask the wrong things, you may seem uninformed or unprepared. But if you ask smart, strategic questions, you come across as someone who is thinking about the long-term, who understands the role on a deeper level, ready to solve this company's problems. A smart interview question does three things: It shows that you've done your research, engages the hiring manager, and reveals that you're being thoughtful in this process. A good question isn't just about getting an answer. It's about framing yourself as a strategic thinker who actually gives a damn about the role.

Consider these two candidates. Candidate A answers every question well but when asked if they have any questions, just says, "No, I think you covered everything." Candidate B engages throughout, then asks, "I noticed that the company recently expanded into a new market. How do you see that impacting this team's priorities over the next year?" Which candidate leaves a stronger impression? The second candidate isn't just responding, they're demonstrating curiosity, awareness, and engagement. They're acting like someone who already belongs at the company.

Generic questions, on the other hand, make you sound like every other candidate. If that's your goal, then go ahead and ask, "What's the company culture like?" or "What does success look like in this role?" (More on the culture question later.) Hiring managers hear these types of questions in every.single.interview. And they usually result in the same generic, rehearsed answers. When you ask generic questions, you get generic answers. Worse, they make you seem like you didn't bother to research the company or think deeply about what you actually want to know.

Speaking as someone who has conducted so many job interviews that I don't even know how to estimate the number anymore, I will tell you that asking questions like that is not a red flag, it's just a no-flag. I'm not going to pass on a candidate because they asked generic questions, but they did waste their moment to do better in a competitive process. If you wouldn't accept a vague, prepackaged answer as a legitimate response to an interview question, why would you expect a vague, prepackaged question to do you any favors?

A Real World Success Story

A candidate once told me about an interview for a senior marketing role at a startup. They had a solid conversation—good answers, good energy—but they could tell the hiring manager wasn't fully sold. Instead of just hoping for the best, they flipped the script and dropped a power move of a question: "If I were to start tomorrow, what's the biggest challenge you'd want me to solve in the first 30 days?" Boom. You could hear the shift in the room. The hiring manager paused, thought for a second, and offered a real answer. It turns out there was a huge misalignment between marketing and sales, and no one had been able to fix it. That was all this candidate needed. The candidate laid out a quick-hit strategy to tackle the issue, connected it to a past experience, and explained how they'd approach it. The result? Offer received.

> **Mike's take:** This wasn't just a good question but an immediate impact question. Most people ask questions about 30-60-90 day success plans, and that's fine. But this candidate was smart. Their strategy was to be less concerned with three months from now and more concerned with how they could impact the company immediately. They didn't just ask a question and move on. They followed up with thoughts and a plan!

The Questions That Make You Look Bad and What to Ask Instead

Most job seekers underestimate how much their own questions shape the hiring manager's perception of them. But make no mistake: the questions you ask tell interviewers who you are, how you think, and how much effort you've put in. Some questions aren't just ineffective. They actively damage your chances of getting the offer. There are three types of bad questions that can turn off a hiring manager instantly:

The Self-Serving Question: These questions scream, "I care about what I can get, not about the job itself." Asking about salary, promotions, or benefits too early makes it seem like you're more interested in what the job can do for you than what you can do for the job. While salary is an important conversation, leading with it is a bad move. Better to frame it strategically during the conversations. I fully believe a company should tell you the salary range before you even speak. And if they don't, it should come up early in conversation. But never let your first question be about salary. It's never a good look. A better option is to ask something like, "Can you tell me about members of the team who have been promoted for their great work?" This works for you because it signals that you're ambitious and focused on delivering results first.

The Lazy Question: These are the questions that show zero effort or research. If you could have found the answer on the company website, in the job description, or with a basic Google search, it's a waste of everyone's time. You should never be in an interview asking, "What does the company do?" or "Who are your biggest competitors?" (Go back to the 10-minute interview prep.) Consider instead: "I noticed [competitor] is making a big push in [x] space. How does your team plan to differentiate?"

The Needy Question: Some questions just put hiring managers in an uncomfortable spot. You may think you're being bold, but really, you're just projecting a lack of confidence. Don't ask, "What made you interview me?" (Who cares? They did! Stop acting surprised!) or "How did I do in this interview?" You're putting them on the spot, and frankly, you sound desperate. Instead, try, "What are the qualities of the most successful hires you've made for this role?" This lets them tell you what they're looking for, without the awkwardness.

A Real World Fail: How One Bad Question Tanked An Interview

A hiring manager once told me about a final-round interview for a high-paying tech role. The candidate crushed the technical portion, had solid experience, and seemed like a strong fit. Then came the Q&A section. The candidate asked, "So, how strict is the company about working hours? Do people actually have to show up on time?" Instant shift in the room. The hiring manager told me, "We were flexible with hours, but that question made it seem like he cared more about finding loopholes than doing great work." The guy went from top candidate to immediate rejection—all because he asked the wrong question at the wrong time.

> **Mike's take:** The questions you ask tell a story. This one screamed, "I don't want to be here" instead of "I want to do great work." If you care about flexibility, ask strategically, "How does the team handle flexibility while collaborating well? You'll get the same answer without making it sound like you're already trying to dodge responsibilities.

Generic questions make you blend in. Thoughtful questions make you stand out. Bad questions signal laziness, disinterest, or desperation. Hiring managers can tell when you're just filling time or checking the box with weak questions. Reframing generic questions into strategic ones makes a huge difference. The best candidates don't just ask questions. They ask really good questions.

The strongest candidates know that an interview isn't just about answering well; it's also about asking well. Your questions tell the interviewer just as much about you as your answers do. So, why waste your chance to make an impression? Make every question count.

Crafting Questions That Lead to Meaningful Conversations

Most candidates ask questions transactionally. They fire one off, get an answer, and move on to the next one. The best candidates use questions to build momentum and create an actual back-and-forth dialogue. Here's how you do it:

- **Start with a broad but targeted question.** For example, "I saw the company recently shifted its focus toward [X]. How is that impacting the team?"
- **Listen carefully to their response.** Revolutionary idea, right? Most candidates don't do this. They're too busy worrying about what they'll ask next.
- **Follow up with a deeper, related question.** Consider, "That's really interesting. How has that shift changed the way your team measures success?"
- **Connect it back to your own experience.** Something like "I actually worked on a similar transition at [previous company]. One of the biggest challenges was x. Has your team run into that?"

Calling this a strategy feels weird because this is just how normal conversations work. I hear all the time from candidates how they wish job interviews were just conversations. To which I say, THEN MAKE IT A DAMN CONVERSATION!

The Mistake of Asking Questions that Feel Scripted

Nothing kills the vibe of an interview like a candidate reading off a list of questions they pulled from an "Ace Your Interview" article five minutes earlier. To be clear, when I say "scripted questions," I don't mean you can't prepare them in advance or write them down. A "scripted question" is a question you could ask on every single interview that isn't adapted or tailored in any way to the conversation you're actually having right now, or the one you're preparing for.

Your questions sound too scripted if: They're too polished. No one naturally says, "Can you describe the key drivers of success for an optimal onboarding experience?" It's too scripted if it doesn't connect to the actual conversation or if it doesn't accomplish anything. Your questions should either help you learn key information or set you up to deliver key information. Pre-scripted questions rarely do this.

How do you fix this? Simply adapt your questions to the specific company and role. Boring and scripted: "What does success look like in this role?" But this is more human, natural, and engaging: "You mentioned that there has been a real disconnect between the sales and marketing departments. Would you say fixing that is an immediate goal for this hire?"

A Simple Framework for Asking Smarter Questions

To ensure your questions are always strategic, use this simple three-step framework:

The Context Hook: Show you've done your research and been listening. Say things like:

- "You mentioned earlier..."
- "I saw on LinkedIn that your team just..."
- "I noticed in the job description that..."

The Core Question: Get to the heart of what you want to know.

- "...how has that impacted your team's priorities?"
- "...how does this role contribute to that shift?"
- "...what challenges have come up as a result?"

The Follow-Up Opportunity: Keep the conversation flowing.

- "That's interesting. Was that an expected challenge, or did it catch the team off guard?"
- "Have you found any unexpected wins from that transition?"
- "How do you see that evolving over the next year?"

Using this framework ensures that your questions feel thoughtful and specific and are engaging.

The bottom line: Mediocre candidates ask surface-level questions and move on. Strong candidates ask questions that drive a real discussion. A great question doesn't just fill time; it shifts the entire interview dynamic into a real conversation. Hiring managers can spot scripted, checkbox-style questions instantly, and nothing kills momentum faster than sounding like you copied and pasted from an online list. The best candidates come prepared, ask smart, engaging questions, and listen well enough to follow up naturally. When it's time to make a hiring decision, the person who made the interview feel like a conversation and not an interrogation is the candidate they'll remember. So, don't waste your shot. Make every question count.

The Culture Question Trap and What to Ask Instead

If you want to sound like every other candidate and learn absolutely nothing, go ahead and ask, "What's the company culture like?" If I had to estimate, I would say that I hear this on about 65% of the interviews I do. The thing is, it literally accomplishes nothing. No one is going to say, "Actually, we're a toxic mess, and you'll hate it here." Instead, they'll serve up a perfectly rehearsed answer about teamwork, innovation, and how it's a good place to be. And you will have learned a total of nothing.

Hiring managers expect this culture question, and they have a prepackaged, fluffy answer ready to go. You're not getting anything useful out of it. Culture has become a bit of an industry buzzword with no real definition. (Yes, I know there is a real definition of culture, just in case that guy who argued with me for like 85 comments that I don't know what culture means is reading.) But culture means something different to everyone. You may think a great culture is a place where everyone is friends and hangs out after work. Someone else may think a great culture is one where they are trusted and not micromanaged. Someone else may just be after places that have video games and rock climbing walls in the office. To this, I say that if you want to know something specific, you have to ask about it specifically.

Whenever a candidate asks me the culture question, I give them a second shot and ask them if there is something specific about "culture" that is important to them so that I can tell them more about it. But most interviewers won't do this. They'll just say it's pretty good and move on. If you really want to know what it's like to work somewhere, you need to ask about real situations, not general concepts. The key is to frame your question in a way that forces the interviewer to provide specific examples instead of vague marketing fluff. Better questions get better answers. Here are a few better questions:

> *"Can you tell me about a recent challenge the team faced and how they handled it?"* This question should elicit an answer that will tell you about the team or company's problem-solving approach, how they collaborate, and about leadership responsiveness.
> *"How does the company recognize employees who go above and beyond?"* This answer to this question should reveal whether hard work is rewarded or just expected.
> *"What are the common traits of people who thrive here?"* This answer should tell you what the company actually values in employees, not just what they say they do.
> *"What's an example of how leadership responded to feedback from employees?"* If they struggle to answer, it's a red flag that leadership doesn't listen.

In this example of a strong exchange, instead of a generic response, the candidate gets some insight into how the company operates under pressure.

Candidate: "Can you tell me about a time when the company faced a challenge that really tested its values?"

Hiring Manager: "Actually, last year, we had to go through a major restructuring, and transparency became key. Leadership held open Q&A sessions every week, and even though not every answer was easy, they made sure employees weren't left in the dark."

Candidate: "That's great to hear. What kind of questions came up the most?"

But a hiring manager's response, or lack thereof, can tell you as much as the answer itself. Here's a red flag of an exchange:

Candidate: "What's an example of how leadership responded to employee feedback?"

Hiring Manager: "Uh, well… I can't think of a specific example, but we're always open to feedback!"

In this example, the hiring manager might as well have just said that leadership ignores feedback. If the hiring manager struggles to come up with real examples, hesitates, or dodges the question, it might be a sign that the culture isn't as great as they claim. They might be covering something up if they don't give specific examples and their answer is vague, overly positive, or full of buzzwords. Did the hiring manager hesitate or squirm at all? If they can't think of an example of how leadership has responded to feedback, that's a red flag. Did they become overly defensive? They might be hiding something if they insist that "Oh, our culture is amazing, no issues at all!"

That said, it is also okay that sometimes people think about a good answer. I try to give good, real answers when candidates ask me good, real questions. But sometimes I want to think about it first. An engaged, thoughtful interviewer who takes the time to compose a good answer when asked a good question is not a red flag.

Asking "What's the company culture like?" is lazy. You'll get a rehearsed answer that tells you nothing. Culture isn't a slogan—it's behavior. The way to uncover the truth is to ask about real situations: how leadership reacts to challenges, how employees are recognized, and how feedback is given. If they struggle to give specifics, that's a red flag. So if you care about culture, don't just ask about it. Make them prove it. If you want a real, insightful answer, ask the specific question (strategically!) about what's important to you.

Asking About Problem-Solving, Collaboration, and Team Dynamics

Most candidates walk into an interview thinking about the role: what they would be responsible for, what they would be expected to deliver. Smart candidates? They think about how the work actually gets done. They know that a job isn't just about checking tasks off a list. It's about how the team functions, how decisions are made, and what happens when things go sideways. Things always go sideways.

It's easy to assume that if you understand the job description, you understand the job, but the same role can feel completely different depending on how teams operate and how the company solves problems. A company that claims to be "fast-paced and innovative" might actually be "disorganized and constantly changing priorities." A company that boasts about "strong leadership" might actually mean that "decisions get made behind closed doors with zero input from the team." Failing to ask about problem-solving, collaboration, and decision-making can lead to some nasty surprises after you start the job.

Here's what can happen when you don't ask how the work gets done. Let's say you join a company that claims to be "fast-moving and agile." But then it turns out that every decision needs approval from five levels of management, aaaaaaand nothing actually moves quickly. Or maybe you accept a role thinking you'll be working with a highly collaborative team only to find out that everyone works in silos, hoards information, and collaboration is just a buzzword on the careers page. Or maybe you think that when challenges come up, the team adapts quickly. In reality, they panic, point fingers, and throw everything on the nearest scapegoat, which, congrats, could be you! Welcome to the team!

To avoid these nightmare scenarios, you need to ask the right questions, the ones that reveal how the work actually gets done. Generic questions about collaboration will get you PR-style answers. Instead of asking, "What's teamwork like here?"—which guarantees a scripted response about "great culture"—ask about specific situations that reveal real insights. Here are examples of good questions and why they work.

Question	Why It Works
"Can you walk me through how the team collaborates on a major project from start to finish?"	Garners a description of actual workflow dynamics, not just a generic "we work well together."
"How are decisions typically made within this team? Can you give me an example of a tough call that had to be made recently?"	Reveals whether decisions are made transparently or dictated from the top without input.
"How does leadership handle disagreements within the team?"	Uncovers whether conflicts are addressed productively or ignored until they explode.
"Can you tell me about a time when the team had to adapt quickly to an unexpected challenge?"	Shows how the company operates under pressure—do they pivot smoothly or spiral into chaos?
"What happens when a project deadline is at risk? How does the team respond?"	Gives insight into whether leadership is supportive or if last-minute crunch mode is the norm.

Consider the following strong exchange that asks them to reveal whether leadership listens to employees or just dictates from the top.

Candidate: "How are major decisions made on this team?"

Hiring Manager: "Well, typically leadership gathers input, but the final call is made at the executive level."

Candidate: "Interesting. Can you give an example of a time when the team pushed for a different approach than leadership expected?"

How a hiring manager answers your questions is just as important as what they say. Did they give specific examples? If they struggled to provide real examples, that's a bad sign. It suggests either a lack of self-awareness or a lack of actual collaboration. Are they honest about challenges? Every team has obstacles. If they insist everything runs perfectly, they're either unaware of their own dysfunction or lying. Do they emphasize teamwork or hierarchy? If all decisions are made top-down, it might mean little room for employee input or innovation.

Your experience in a job isn't just about your own work. It's also about how the team actually operates. Asking about problem-solving, collaboration, and decision-making helps you uncover hidden challenges or problems before you accept an offer. Instead of asking generic questions about teamwork, get the hiring managers to describe real situations. Pay attention to how they answer—if they dodge specifics, that's a red flag. A strong team can make a tough job enjoyable. A dysfunctional team can make a dream job miserable. Before you accept an offer, make sure you know what you're signing up for.

THE BEST QUESTIONS MIKE HAS EVER BEEN ASKED

Hiring managers hear the same recycled questions hundreds of times. If they can answer your question on autopilot while mentally compiling their grocery list, you've lost your shot at being memorable. The best questions stand out because they create a real discussion, show you've done your research, and maybe even reframe the hiring manager's perspective. The right strong question can help them picture you in the role. A great question forces the interviewer to pause, reflect, and provide a thoughtful answer. Smart candidates ask about specifics: company initiatives, leadership styles, and recent industry shifts. Here are some of the best questions I have ever heard and why they worked.

Question	Why It Worked
"If you could wave a magic wand and fix one problem on your team overnight, what would it be?"	This one gets the hiring manager to reveal the team's biggest pain points and offer insight into the team's current, real challenges.
"Can you tell me about someone who was in this role before and what made them successful?"	Instead of getting generic "success metrics," you get an actual case study of a former employee's successes.

Question	Why It Worked
"When was the last time leadership had to make a tough decision, and how did they communicate it to the team?"	Uncovers leadership transparency, decision-making style, and company culture—without directly asking the generic "What's the culture like?"
"What's something about this role that isn't in the job description but is crucial for success?"	The answer will reveal the unspoken expectations of the job.
"If you were to look back on this hire a year from now, what would make you say, 'That was a great decision'?"	Encourage the hiring manager to picture you as the successful hire.

A good question doesn't just give you information. It tells the hiring manager that you are looking for a great fit in a new job and a role you will be successful in, which is ultimately what every manager wants.

The Bottom Line:

Hiring someone onto a team is a big decision, and as much as we, as job seekers, want to say, "Oh, just take a chance on me," let's be real. Managers' jobs depend on their hires. They also report to a boss and have targets to hit. The money they may offer you is not their personal money but money that it's their job to manage well. Asking good questions shows them that a) you are trying to find the right place to work and b) you will be a safe investment for them if they hire you.

Asking Behavioral Questions: My Most Controversial Interview Advice

I don't like to brag. LOL. JK, of course I do! Here it is: There is one piece of interview advice I give that has gone viral over and over again, tens of millions of views, numerous media articles, and even a career coach who stole the video word-for-word. Yeah, I had to call it out publicly. This advice is not for everyone, and certainly not for people who think all the power should lie with the interviewer! It involves some risk and definitely falls into the playing-to-win category. Here it is: I think you should ask your interviewers and hiring managers behavioral-based interview questions. People don't realize they can do this and how beneficial it can be.

You need to read the room and understand the kind of manager you are interviewing with, but some managers will be blown away if you ask questions like: Can you tell me about someone who was on your team that you helped advance in their career? Can you tell me about a time you managed a dispute between two coworkers and the role you played? Can you tell me about the last person on your team who didn't work out and what you think led to that result?

These are questions that will help you learn about your manager and about the culture. Managers want to know how you work and the behaviors you exhibit at work. You should want to know how they manage and the behaviors they show while managing.

Yes, there will be managers who say things like "Whoa, who is interviewing who here?" Yes, there will be managers who think you sound like a problem or will be difficult to manage. Yes, they do have to really like you for this to work. But, yes, most importantly, being bold like this will make you stand out.

This isn't a magical solution, but know that every time I post about this strategy, the comments are usually job seekers saying, "This won't work, and I won't try it," and hiring managers saying, "I wish people would do this more." Make of that what you will.

Mike's Snarky Do's and Don'ts of Asking Smart Questions

DO ask questions that make the hiring manager think. If they pause before answering, congrats—you just got them to engage instead of reciting the same script they've given to 27 other candidates.

DO make them visualize you in the role. Questions like "If I started tomorrow, what's the first big challenge you'd want me to tackle?" help them picture you in the role. That's what you want.

DO dig for real insights. Instead of asking "What's the company culture like?" ask "Can you tell me about a time when the team had to handle a major challenge?" That will show you how things really work.

DON'T be scared to challenge them. Good managers want good employees. Good employees are not scared to stand out.

DON'T make it all about you. If your first question is about salary, promotions, or benefits, you might as well just say, "I don't actually care about this job. I just want a paycheck." At least pretend to be interested in the work first.

DON'T read off a script like a malfunctioning chatbot. If you ask questions that sound like you copied and pasted them from a LinkedIn article titled "The Ten Best Questions to Ask in an Interview," hiring managers will tune you out immediately. Be genuine, and be in conversation.

CHAPTER EIGHT

Just Send the Damn Follow-Up

TL;DR

Most people either don't follow up after interviews or do it so badly that they might as well not bother. This chapter will teach you how to follow up strategically without coming across as desperate or annoying.

Here's Why You Need To Send A Follow-Up Note

We need to talk about what happens after you leave that interview room, when you're obsessively checking your inbox every 17 seconds, telling yourself, "I'm sure they'll reach out if they want me." Spoiler alert: that's not how this works. The candidates who land jobs aren't necessarily the most qualified. They're the ones who know how to stay visible without giving off stalker vibes. This chapter is your guide to that delicate dance of post-interview communication, where one well-timed email can keep you in the running, but one too many can get your resume filed directly in the digital trash.

Let me tell you a story to illustrate my point. I was about two weeks into a brand new job and had my first post-interview debrief meeting with the hiring team. (At most companies, the process after an interview is for everyone who spoke with the candidate to get together and talk about their feedback.) I have seen these meetings sway things for or against a candidate once everyone starts talking, and they are an important part of hiring. In this case, I was in a room with the VP of sales, a senior sales engineer, and the chief people officer of the company as we were hiring for a high-level sales role.

As we discussed the two final candidates, it was very clear that all three members of the hiring team loved them both, and picking one to hire was going to be hard. As the conversation around the little differences between the candidates was picking up, the senior sales engineer pointed out that one candidate reached out to them after the interview with a follow-up email, and the other did not, which made him prefer the first candidate. The VP of sales responded with the same feedback and said that they also preferred the first candidate because of this.

I had trouble staying quiet (shocker, I know) because, personally, I hate when managers get swayed by things like this, so I started asking questions to hopefully get us back to the conversation about the candidates' skills. Was the first candidate actually better? Will they be a better employee? Does sending an email after an interview actually correlate with being the better hire? I was hoping to get through to everyone, but as a new employee, that rarely happens, not to mention that once the CPO weighed in and agreed, sending emails that sending the follow-up email is "more professional" and a good sign, the decision was made.

That meeting has stuck with me for a bunch of reasons, but a big takeaway was that no matter how much you may hate it, or how many recruiters beg managers not to make decisions based on ideas like this, that is what's happening behind closed doors. Honestly, even with the doors open. Most people are not secretive about how things like that influence their decisions. I have seen hiring managers assume that somebody isn't interested in the job or not engaged enough with the company over a lack of these emails. I have even seen somebody assume that the candidate may have taken another offer because they didn't inquire about next steps after the interview. The hiring world is strange, and I have seen these strange behaviors from otherwise great managers. So, on that day, I started telling job seekers the same thing I'm telling you right now: JUST SEND THE FOLLOW-UP!

The theme of this book has been and continues to be: do all this to increase your chances of getting hired and paying your bills, and stop complaining that you shouldn't have to do it because that won't help. So here it is again. It's shocking to me how many candidates either skip this step entirely or send generic thank-you notes that add zero value, even when they know some managers make decisions based on this kind of thing. And trust me, just because they make a hiring decision for a dumb reason, does not mean they are a bad manager or that it's a bad place to work. You have to stop telling yourself this.

The Dangerous Myth of "If They Want Me, They'll Reach Out"

Here's a hard truth: doing nothing after an interview is one of the biggest mistakes you can make. Many job seekers tell themselves, "If they want to talk to me more, they'll get in touch," and then wonder why they've been ghosted.

I have bad news for all of you: none of us is the main character of this story. While, in your mind, a manager is not getting back to you because they hate you or are terrible at their job, it's also possible that they had two candidates reschedule their interviews and had to reschedule another three for their own reasons, delaying the process by two weeks. Or maybe they're just drowning in work, approvals, or internal politics. (You know what I'm talking about. Don't pretend that you don't.) Or they're busy reading great follow-up emails from other candidates and deciding that their follow-up email makes them the better candidate. (Barf, I know.) Now, this does not mean that you should chase the hiring manager, and it definitely does not mean that you should beg. I'm begging you, please don't beg! But it does mean you can not skip this step.

Follow-Up Fail

Here's a stupid-but-real hiring truth: While some managers really care if you send a thank-you note, others will let an unimpressive thank-you note end your candidacy. There is zero data proving that a thank-you email correlates with whether you're a great hire or not, but does that stop some hiring managers from letting it influence their decisions? Nope.

I had a hiring manager pass on a candidate once because the email they sent after the interview had a typo. The manager said, "This was the most important email they were going to write today, and they didn't even proofread it." (Eye roll.)

Mike's take: This is why you play the game. You're not proving that you can send an email. You're making sure you check a possible box a manager has, and taking one more opportunity to make yourself look good. More on that soon. You can call it dumb, but it's real. Do the thing to get the job!

When you don't follow up, you're missing a huge opportunity to tip the scales in your favor. Hiring managers aren't just looking for qualified candidates; they're looking for candidates who actually want the job. And beyond that, when you do this properly, this is yet another great opportunity to sell yourself into the job.

The Fine Line Between Strategic Follow-Up and Borderline Harassment

Before you start firing off messages, let's talk about what effective follow-up actually looks like. There's a critical difference between showing genuine interest and coming across as desperate. Here's what hiring managers think. You can see where it gets to be too much.

Follow-Up Style	Hiring Manager Reaction
One thoughtful email	"Nice. They're engaged and professional."
Second follow-up after a week	"Still reasonable."
Third email with a "Just checking in again..."	"This is feeling a little desperate."
LinkedIn message, plus a call	"Oh no."
Commenting on their Instagram post	"Security?"

Follow-Up Fail

One time, I saw a candidate absolutely kill their own chances with over-the-top follow-ups. The candidate sent three emails in five days, DMed the hiring manager on LinkedIn, DMed people on the manager's team asking if the manager was working, and emailed information about their current company that they should have kept secret to the manager in an attempt to impress him. Big mistake.

The hiring manager actually liked this person... until they started acting like a bill collector. Eventually, I had to just send a polite rejection email to make them go away. The kicker? They were absolutely a top candidate until they demonstrated both a lack of professionalism and far too little patience.

The Perfect Post-Interview Follow-Up Message

Here's the truth most career advice won't tell you: Your follow-up email isn't just a polite formality. It's a strategic move that can actually tip the scales in your favor. I've seen thousands of follow-up messages in my career, and I can tell you with certainty that most candidates make the same critical mistakes. They either send bland, forgettable notes that could have been written by AI, or they pester hiring managers with endless check-ins that scream, "I'm anxious!" How do you actually do this? Let's break it down.

You send one, maybe two messages max, then move on. This isn't just about being polite. It's about psychology. When you bombard a hiring manager with follow-ups, you're not being enthusiastic—you're being desperate. And desperation has never landed anyone their dream job. And the timing really matters.

Timing	Impression
Within 24 hours	Perfect timing. Shows you're engaged but not desperate.
After 48 hours	Still fine, but don't push it further.
After a week	Might be okay for a second follow-up, but you're on thin ice.
After two weeks	They've moved on. You should too.

I once worked with a candidate—let's call him Alex—who sent a thoughtful follow-up the day after his interview, reinforcing his value to the team. The hiring manager mentioned in their feedback that his email stood out because it wasn't just a generic "Thanks for your time" message. Compare that to another candidate who sent six—yes, SIX—follow-up emails over two weeks. The hiring manager confided in me that they were actually leaning toward making an offer to the latter candidate until this bright red flag popped up. To the hiring manager, it signaled a lack of professional boundaries and a lack of confidence in their own candidacy.

SIDEBAR

Okay, look, I know some of these stories may elicit a "WTF are you serious!?!?!" response from you. And I do wish that I'd made them up for the book, but they are real-life things that happen in the hiring world every day. I can advise managers that stuff like this is silly. That's part of my job, but have you tried to change someone's mind recently? That s#@t is not easy!

When I tell these stories, it may be really easy to dismiss them and say something like "Whatever. I'm dodging a bullet not working for that person," (and there are 50 job search creators who will tell you the same thing,) but the truth is that may not really be the case. Remember the chapter about not letting everything be a red flag? Some people simply aren't great at hiring, or have weird decision criteria but make amazing managers. And some companies have a wonderful culture and benefit plan but maybe don't do a great job training their interviewers and hiring managers. Nothing is perfect in this world, and that includes your next job. So instead of letting some guru convince you that you don't need to do any of this stuff, that all you need is their course for $899 to land a job, just know that people are going to be people and that this is the stuff happening behind most closed doors. You can accept it and try to get the job, or we can go viral on TikTok talking about how we refuse to. I know which one I pick whenever I'm on the job market.

Reinforce Your Value, Not Just Your Gratitude

Be real. Thank-you notes are not magic job-winning spells. If you bombed the interview, a stellar thank-you note won't save you. But when you're neck-and-neck with another candidate, a strategic thank-you note could break the tie and push you ahead. (Refer to the first story in the chapter. It's real!) Most candidates treat thank-you notes as a box to check, a quick "Thanks for your time!" email they send because someone told them they should. That's a wasted opportunity. Instead of seeing this as a formality, think of it as one last strategic play to reinforce why you're the perfect fit.

A generic thank-you email is about as memorable as a handshake at a networking event. Nice, but completely forgettable. Here's the text of a totally forgettable thank-you note: "Hi [Hiring Manager], Thanks for taking the time to chat today. I really appreciate it. Looking forward to the next steps!" Compare that to this much more strategic one:

> Hi [Hiring Manager],
>
> I really appreciated our conversation about [specific topic]. Our discussion about [specific challenge] stuck with me, and I'd love the opportunity to bring my experience in [relevant skill] to your team. Looking forward to next steps and the possibility of contributing to [Company Name].
>
> Sincerely,
> [Your name]

The difference? One is generic. It tells them nothing about why they should hire you. The second one reinforces the candidate's value, reminding the interviewers that you're the right person for the job, keeping you fresh in their minds, just as they're making their decision. A good follow-up should be:

Personalized: References a specific conversation or insight from the interview.
Value-driven: Reinforces how you would solve *their* problems.
Concise: Gets to the point without rambling.
Professional but authentic: Sounds like a real human, not a corporate robot.
Have a forward-thinking close: Express enthusiasm without sounding desperate.
Here's what makes for a bad follow-up:
Generic: "Thank you for your time. I look forward to hearing from you." (Yawn. Delete.)
Needy: "Just checking in again to see if you've made a decision?" (They didn't forget to hire you.)
Too long: Nobody is reading your second cover letter disguised as a follow-up. (I'm admittedly very guilty of this one, though.)
Overly formal: "I hereby wish to express my sincere gratitude for the opportunity to discuss the aforementioned position…" (Congratulations, you own a thesaurus.)

Here is the follow-up formula that actually works:

Section	What to Include	Reasoning
Subject Line	Keep it simple: "Thank you for your time – [title of role]"	Clear and professional, easy to find in a cluttered inbox.
Opening	Thank them and reference something specific from your conversation.	Shows you were engaged and paying attention.
Value Add	Reinforce how you'd solve their specific challenge.	Reminds them why they need YOU specifically.
Closing	Express enthusiasm and clear next steps.	Makes their job easier by being direct about expectations.

Real World Thank You Notes

THE GOOD:

Subject: Thank you – Marketing Manager position

Hi Sarah,

I really appreciated our conversation yesterday about the challenges your team is facing with the upcoming product launch. Your insights about needing someone who can bridge the gap between technical features and customer benefits really resonated with me.

After our talk, I was thinking about the campaign strategy we discussed. In my role at XYZ Company, we faced a similar challenge with technical products, and I was able to increase conversion rates by 32% by focusing on customer-centric storytelling rather than feature lists. I'd be excited to bring that same approach to your team.

I'm looking forward to the next steps in the process. If you need any additional information from me in the meantime, please don't hesitate to reach out.

Best,
Mike

THE BAD:

Subject: Thanks!

Hi there,

Thanks for interviewing me yesterday for the marketing position. I enjoyed our conversation and learning more about your company. The role sounds great, and I think I would be a good fit.

Looking forward to hearing back from you soon.

Thanks again,
Michael

THE CRINGEWORTHY:

Subject: I NEED THIS JOB!!!

Jessica, I cannot thank you enough for yesterday's interview opportunity. This position would be absolutely LIFE-CHANGING for me and my family. I've been searching for the perfect role for eight months now, and I just KNOW this is it.

I promise I will work harder than anyone you've ever hired. I'll come in early, stay late, work weekends—whatever it takes! You won't regret giving me this chance.

I've been checking my email every five minutes, hoping to hear back. Please let me know your decision as soon as possible. I have been losing sleep over this opportunity.

Desperately hoping to join your team,
Michael

Confession Time. Watch Me Do It Wrong.

Okay, I'm going to share something with you because, believe it or not, I'm not perfect! I have done that last one on a level more extreme than even my made-up example! The reason I write about it and call it cringeworthy isn't to make fun of you if you're doing it; it's because I still cringe thinking about how desperate I once was for a specific job and how I absolutely cost myself the role with my neediness.

The following are a few real emails (edited for length and private information) that I sent to a potential manager during the hiring process. To set the stage, the emails I've included are only the emails where I was being extra needy, not normal conversational emails back and forth during the process, though I keep track of how many emails I sent this person for you:

Email 1 (Friday after the first interview):

Hi (Manager),

I wanted to send you a quick note heading into the weekend thanking you not only for the time today but for the thought you've already put into this role and process. Even if my candidacy were to end here—I really hope it doesn't—I'd take some lessons from the notion document you sent out in advance and be appreciative of how many details I was given before ever having to ask for them.

That being said, I also wanted to be clear that I walked away from the call excited about this opportunity and felt like there was a lot of alignment between [Company] and not only my background and skill set but also my general approach to talent acquisition. With a sudden layoff, there is always a line to straddle between finding the ideal role vs. just getting back to work, but it felt great to talk about a role that, at least after an early conversation, felt like the type of opportunity I am really looking for next in my career. It isn't just having some industry knowledge already that makes me say that (people can learn any new industry if they want to), but the passion for good recruiting being the first step in building a good culture that you seem to agree with. I think my experience, approach, and mindset align well with what you are all building, and the hybrid, not-quite-figured-out-yet role is often where I thrive.

I know the market is full of talented people right now and that you will be speaking with many of them, but I do hope we can continue the conversation soon.

Thanks again and have a great weekend!
Mike Peditto

P.S. I usually don't do this, and feel a bit cheesy that I am, but I wanted to just share a comment that a former coworker had left on my LinkedIn. I'm sharing this specifically because I appreciate her noticing how important it was for me to really ingrain myself in my former company by learning and knowing all I could about the company. I've always felt this is a key to building trust quickly and being viewed as a real business partner rather than just another recruiter.

Email 2 (Tuesday):

I wanted to check and see how some of your calls are going for the role and if you have had a chance to think about our conversation and if it makes sense to continue in the interview process.

I know you are incredibly busy with interviews, and I don't envy managers having to pick candidates out of so many applicants, but I am really excited about the alignment I felt between this opportunity and my specific skill sets and desires for a new role, and would love the chance to continue exploring it by talking about some problem-solving like your note mentioned as the next step.

I hope you have a happy Thanksgiving and look forward to what I hope are some next steps soon.

Thanks,
Mike

Email 5 (A follow-up after my second interview)

I just got to meet with [employee-x] and liked hearing from her about the different teams and many projects she is leading right now and what her needs are for the team.

She mentioned the next steps would be setting a follow-up time with you. With timing being a potential issue, I could have the project I was asked to do finished and be free anytime tomorrow if that is not too soon for her or too quick of a turnaround to schedule. If not tomorrow, I could also be free on Monday anytime from 11–1 CST.

If you need any more availability, please let me know as well.

Thanks for all of your help so far in the process. I'm looking forward to the next steps!

Email 9 (sending availability for the final interview on a Friday):

That's exciting to hear! I appreciate such fast feedback as well.

I'll make myself available as needed to speak with them, as I know how difficult coordinating schedules can be, especially with an offsite involved.

If Thursday works, I will make Thursday work. If off hours or weird times work, I will make those work too. Just let me know what works best, and it'll be fine. I'd love for the world to rotate around me, but I guess it just doesn't!

Good luck in your race this weekend!

Email 10 (Monday):

I hope the race went well and that you are not nursing too many sore muscles. I write this with a compression sleeve around my quad, as the kind of accident-prone person who can not go a week at the gym without injuring something else!

I just wanted to double-check if you were able to find a time that works to speak with [final interviewer] this week. I know what their schedules probably look like, so I definitely want to be sure I am available for them and get the time blocked. Like I mentioned, I can do some weird times or scheduling games to make it work if you have a few suggestions of when they are available, whatever works best for everyone on your end.

Thanks again for all of your help in staying on top of all of this the last few weeks. I'm excited to meet them!

Email 12 (Thursday, immediately after final interview)

Hi, one more thank you email from me!

I know how overwhelmed hiring teams are everywhere right now, and you keep unnecessarily apologizing for delays, but I only applied three weeks ago today and had my first interview a day after that. (Ask me again about how much I love tracking data and spreadsheets!) I would consider this a smooth process even in a precedented time—if that even still exists—let alone a time where you get 1000 applicants to a recruiter role, so thank you for keeping things running well and for the time and late hours you've put into it. Honestly, it says a lot of good things to me about a potential next manager!

I know you mentioned having a few candidates to get through and wanting to wrap the role up this week, but to continue being as transparent as possible, as I've been this whole time, this is the opportunity I want, and truly I believe that this is the right match for both myself and the company. I think I have started to build a good rapport in a short time with everyone I have met so far in the process and would be excited to partner and work with them. I understand a lot of the goals and challenges of this role and see where I bring immediate value, as well as where there are opportunities for me to continue growing and expanding my abilities along with the company.

There is a strong alignment between the company's mission and values, how I operate personally and professionally, and what I want out of a next role, and I'm confident that I can help play a key role in [company's] future. No matter what happens, thank you again for a good interviewing experience, but hopefully, there are a lot more conversations to come between us!

Mike

Email 13 (Friday, YES THE NEXT DAY!)

Apologies for another email! I wanted to check in with you as I'm wrapping up some end-of-week things. Yesterday, I know you mentioned potentially making an offer today, and I'm, of course, still very interested in this role and [company] and feel confident in the addition I'd be. Will we be able to connect sometime today?

Thanks

Mike's take: WOOF! I know you may read this and say it's not that bad, but imagine all of these long emails begging for updates and the job when you are also running a large team, hiring for several roles, and dealing with hundreds of candidates. There are some pros to this email chain for sure: I'm professional. I clearly understand the team's needs and show interest. When they needed info from me, they got it immediately. (Those are the emails I didn't include here.) But here's what else was on display: I was desperate. Nobody wants to be begged. I lacked patience. Following up after not hearing back within a day is not the way to play this. I was wordy. Just because you make jokes about being long-winded doesn't make it okay. And I gave this person no space. Did you catch the part where this was all happening over Thanksgiving, and I was still looking for an answer?

Anyway, if you're wondering, I finally got a call back after that last email on a Friday with the rejection. Can I say for sure that all of these emails cost me the job? Of course not, and even if they did cost me the job, the company would never admit it. But I feel confident that if it had been down to me and one other person and we were both very qualified and good fits, it becomes much easier to hire the person who feels more calm, cool, and collected and a bit less pushy and desperate, right?

When They Go Silent or How to Follow Up Without Being Pushy

Let's talk about the ghosting phenomenon in job interviews. You crushed the interview, sent a solid follow-up, and now… nothing. Crickets. Silence doesn't always mean rejection, and it also doesn't mean you should keep sending emails until they cave.

The truth is that hiring processes are messy. Companies can be disorganized, priorities shift, and communication falls through the cracks. Before you spiral into self-doubt, consider these scenarios: The timeline they gave has passed. The hiring manager said they would get back to you by Friday, and now it's Monday. This is actually common. Decision-makers get pulled into meetings, approvals get delayed, and sometimes they're just waiting on one slow-moving executive to weigh in. Or maybe they're still actively interviewing candidates. Companies often want to meet all the candidates before making decisions. Your interview might have gone great, but they're comparing you to other candidates they haven't even interviewed yet. Internal priorities may have shifted. Sometimes, hiring gets put on pause because of budget freezes, reorganizations, or other internal chaos. Finally, maybe your contact is out of office. Never underestimate the power of poorly timed vacations, illness, or personal emergencies to disrupt hiring timelines.

But there are times that radio silence probably does mean that you're out. Did they use vague language about next steps? Have you followed up twice and gotten no response? If the job posting disappeared but you haven't heard anything, you are probably out. You're probably also out if your follow-ups were answered with only increasingly delayed vague responses. Sorry. I get this question all the time: "They said I'd hear back by Friday, and it's been three weeks. What does that mean?" Sorry to say it, but I'll hold your hand as I do: You're out. You got ghosted. They just weren't that into you!

Here is a formula for writing a polite, not-annoying nudge:

Section	What to Include	Example
Subject Line	Keep it short and professional.	"Following Up – [title of role]"
Opening Line	Reference previous conversation and express continued interest.	"I hope you're doing well! Just wanted to follow up on our conversation about [title of role]."
Value Reminder	Reiterate a specific strength or contribution.	"I'm really excited about the opportunity to bring my experience in [specific skill] to your team."
Closing	Ask about next steps, but leave it open-ended.	"Looking forward to hearing any updates when you have them. Let me know if I can provide any additional information."

Example 1: First Follow-Up After Interview

Subject: Following Up - Marketing Coordinator Interview

Hi Taylor,

I hope your week is going well. I wanted to follow up on our conversation last Thursday about the Marketing Coordinator position. I really enjoyed learning about how your team is approaching the upcoming campaign season.

After our discussion about the challenges of coordinating across multiple channels, I'm even more excited about the possibility of bringing my experience with integrated marketing to your team.

I understand the hiring process takes time. When you have a moment, could you share any updates on the timeline for next steps?

Thank you again for your time and consideration.

Best regards,
Jamie

Example 2: Second Follow-Up (After No Response)

Subject: Checking In - Social Media Manager Position

Hi Alex,

I hope you're doing well. I'm reaching out to check if there have been any developments regarding the Social Media Manager position we discussed on March 1st.

I remain very interested in the role and the opportunity to help elevate your brand's social presence, especially given my experience with similar audience growth challenges we discussed.

I understand this is a busy time. If you have any updates when you have a moment, I'd appreciate hearing from you.

Thank you,
Riley

The harsh reality is that sometimes, after you've followed up, no response really is your answer. One thing I say all the time is that companies treat their top candidates like top candidates. They didn't forget you existed if they were planning to hire you. If you're waiting for weeks, it's because, at best, they're keeping you as a backup, but the reality is that they have probably moved on and just went into Casper mode. Of course, there is a difference between a slow-moving process where things are a bit delayed and being totally blown off, and it's important to understand that. One key is communication. Are you being updated? Do you know where things stand? Or are you constantly begging for attention and answers? I've been there myself. There was a role I *really* wanted, and after what felt like a great interview, they said, "We'll be in touch by the end of the week." Guess what? Silence. I followed up once and got a vague, "We're still finalizing things." A week later? Another vague update. This went on for three more weeks until I finally got the rejection email. At that point, I already knew.

If they really want you, you're almost never left wondering. Write one follow-up, maybe two. But if they keep stringing you along? Assume you're Plan B, C, D, or Z and that it's time to move on. As they say: if they wanted to, they would.

What Does Moving On Mean?

When do I move on after an interview? is a question I get asked a lot. The real answer is immediately/ What are you even waiting for?! Keep searching! But I know that question really means, "When should I give up on getting the job?"

I think this question stems from people wanting to send a "you can't dump me, I dumped you" email and feel like they won, but the truth is, I don't think you should do that. When I hear someone ask when to move on, I wonder what moving on really means. The reason I say that you should move on immediately is that until you have a job, you still don't have a job. And if you are an active job seeker, you should be focused on finding the next opportunity, not waiting on this one.

Instead of breaking up with the job, realize when two weeks have gone by without having heard back, it's time to recategorize this prospect from "active possibilities" to "completed applications" and continue doing all the stuff you should have been doing during those two weeks anyway. This isn't just organizational; it's a psychological release that creates mental space for new opportunities.

And hey, if they come back to you a month later apologizing and saying they'd love to move forward with you, the ball is now in your court. Maybe you're still interested. Maybe you've landed somewhere else. Or maybe you took the long silence as a sign to just write them off. But that choice is yours. Listen to what you are being told with the silence, keep moving forward, and cross whatever bridge shows up later. Don't waste your time worrying about what "moving on" means.

The Long-Game Follow-Up

Stop me if you've heard this one before: "We will keep you in mind for future opportunities" or something similar. Okay, just kidding, don't stop me. I want to keep going, but I know you've heard it and you don't believe it. But what if I told you that I've both gotten a job and hired people based on previous interviews that didn't work out? Is it rare? Of course! But it can happen, and so you should always try to walk away on a good note. It could absolutely happen to you.

Just because you weren't the top choice today doesn't mean you won't be the best option tomorrow. Hiring managers don't love rejecting good candidates. In fact, they often wish they had multiple openings. The candidate they chose might not work out, which happens plenty. New roles open up all the time, and hiring managers prefer candidates they already know.

A few years back, I had a great round of interviews for a role, and it felt like the perfect fit. Unfortunately, they wound up hiring someone else, though the manager was very clear that they wished they could hire two people and that picking one was hard. She said that we should stay in touch because you never know. We exchanged pleasant emails. I would check in with her from time to time. (Remember all those networking tips earlier?) And one day, she eventually asked me if I'd be open to a contract role for some projects they were working on. I was doing some consulting at the time, so I excitedly said yes and wound up working there for quite a while. She really did want me to be on the team. This does happen!

The goal of the long-game follow-up strategy isn't to remind them that they rejected you—it's to position yourself as an ongoing, valuable connection. The best time to follow up is three to six months after your initial interview, when new roles might be opening up. Here's how to write this email:

Section	What to Include	Example
Subject Line	Keep it light and professional	"Checking in – excited to stay in touch"
Opening Line	Reference past interaction	"I hope you're doing well. I wanted to follow up after our conversation about [past role]."
Update	Share what you've been working on since	"Since we last spoke, I've been leading [specific project] and refining my skills in [relevant area]."
Reconnection Ask	Express interest in future roles	"I'd love to stay in touch and hear about any upcoming opportunities on your team."

Here is an example of a great follow-up note a few months after an initial rejection:

Subject: Checking In – excited to stay in touch

Hi [Hiring Manager's Name],

Hope you're doing well! I wanted to follow up after our conversation about the [be specific here] role a few months back. I really enjoyed learning more about [company name] and the work your team is doing.

Since we last spoke, I've been leading [specific project] and deepening my expertise in [relevant skill]. I'd love to stay in touch and hear about any upcoming opportunities that might be a good fit. Please don't hesitate to reach out if anything comes up. I'd be excited to contribute to your team.

Best,
[Your Name]

Following up isn't just about keeping your name in their inbox. You really do need to time it right. Too soon, and you seem pushy. Too often? You seem desperate. But the right message at the right time? That can put you back on their radar just when they need someone like you. The trick is knowing when to re-engage strategically as opposed to when simply to move on with your dignity intact. If you handled the initial follow-up well but didn't get the offer, you might still have a shot months down the line, but only if you play it smart. The best times to reach out are:

Three to six months after rejection as teams re-evaluate hiring needs. Companies reshuffle priorities all the time, and hiring managers would much rather reach out to someone they already know than start from scratch.
If you see a new opening at the company that fits your skills. If they're hiring for a role similar to the one you interviewed for, it's worth reconnecting, especially if you made a strong impression the first time.
When the company shares news that's relevant to you. A funding round, a leadership change, an expansion all create new opportunities that didn't exist before. Reaching out now shows you're paying attention and still interested.

Bad times to reach out are:

Right after being rejected. Rejections sting, but don't immediately turn around and ask if they've changed their mind. Give it time.
Every few weeks, asking if they've reconsidered. This isn't a customer service complaint where persistence wears them down. If they haven't responded, that's your answer.
With a long-winded explanation of why they made a mistake rejecting you. Even if you know you were the better candidate, trying to argue your way back in is a bad look.

Your goal is to position yourself as a valuable connection. Your follow-up should feel casual, professional, and genuinely interested in the company's success. If you're checking in after a few months, focus on what's changed since you last spoke. Maybe you've completed a big project, taken on a leadership role, or developed a new skill that makes you an even stronger fit. Your message should subtly say, *"I'm even better now than when you interviewed me."*

I rejected a candidate for a social media manager role as we were down to a final three and had to make a really hard decision. In a perfect world, I'd have hired all three, but we don't live in a perfect world. The candidate connected with me on LinkedIn and continued to be an active user as we engaged with each other occasionally, back and forth. Eventually, she reached out to tell me how she had really been working on her LinkedIn presence, showing me some data reflecting her growth and experimentation and asked if we have any openings since we last spoke. My company had been discussing adding a new role to our social media team, and I brought her up with the team's manager, who also remembered her fondly. I set the two of them up for an interview, and she was able to join the team shortly after. Again, this does happen!

When done right, a well-timed follow-up can land you a job you didn't even know was available. But the key is patience. Chasing after a company that's already moved on is a waste of your time. Know when to reach out, when to step back, and most importantly, when to redirect your energy to the next great opportunity.

Mike's Snarky Do's and Don'ts of Just Send The Damn Follow-Up

DO send one thoughtful follow-up within 24 hours that references specific interview points and reinforces your value.

DO wait about a week before sending a second follow-up if you haven't heard back.

DO know when to take the hint. If they've ghosted you after two follow-ups, it's time to move on.

DO consider playing the long game with a strategic check-in three to six months later.

DON'T bombard them with messages across multiple platforms.

DON'T show up at their office unannounced or start commenting on their personal social media.

DON'T send that passive-aggressive "I guess you're not interested" email.

DON'T take silence personally. Sometimes it's really not about you. It's about their chaotic internal processes.

Remember: Following up isn't about begging for attention. It's about strategically reinforcing your value at exactly the right moments. Master this delicate art, and you'll be the candidate they remember when future decisions are being made.

CHAPTER NINE

The Truth About Negotiation

TL;DR

Salary negotiation isn't a high-stakes battle between enemies. It's a conversation between future teammates trying to find alignment. This chapter urges readers to stop taking advice from people with no skin in the game and instead approach negotiations with awareness, empathy, and strategy. The key to earning more isn't always about demanding more money—it's about getting comfortable talking about money, understanding total compensation (including equity, PTO, benefits, and flexibility), and recognizing when negotiation is appropriate and when it's not. Being flexible, informed, and respectful is far more effective than playing hardball or following outdated, one-size-fits-all advice.

Before We Begin

Before talking about negotiation, I want to be clear about something. Most of the salary negotiation advice you hear online sucks! It's well intentioned, it doesn't suck on purpose, but there is a problem with all salary negotiation advice, and that includes mine. Nobody giving it to you has any stakes in the outcome! When people tell you that you should "always negotiate," they ignore the fact that sometimes negotiating backfires and you may lose your offer. Except when they hear that story, they say something like "Wow, you dodged a bullet" because it doesn't impact them in any way that their extreme "always negotiate" advice cost you an offer.

There are two things I want you to take away from this chapter, whether or not you take any of my advice:

- People who are comfortable talking about money make more money. Full stop. If you are uncomfortable talking about money, start getting comfortable with it. People who aren't scared of tough topics get more in life.
- Salary negotiation is not a battle between adversaries. It is two sides trying to wind up playing for the same team. Do not enter them contentiously.

Remember that all negotiation advice (including mine) is not one size fits all. I'm equipping you with tools to hopefully earn more money, not an instruction manual to follow. Stick to what you are comfortable doing, and always read the room and the situation. There are no universal negotiation tips. I'm trying to give you some general advice here, so PLEASE, above all else, DON'T BE STUPID!

Beyond Salary Games

When people think of negotiation, they imagine a dramatic, high-stakes salary standoff, a hiring manager on one side, the candidate on the other, tension thick in the air as they battle over a few thousand dollars. If you only take away one lesson from this chapter, let it be this: *Everybody in a negotiation wants the same thing!* This is not a 1980s boardroom. This is not a movie. This is just a regular-a$$ Tuesday at the computer in a button-pushing office, between a manager and a recruiter, and they both want you for the open role on their team.

Let's take the stakes down a bit when we talk about negotiation. Stop thinking about it as you versus. them. The question you need to ask yourself is not how to win in a negotiation but how to create a situation where you and the company both win, especially the recruiter. If I could give every candidate we wanted to hire a billion dollars, trust me, I would! Recruiters and managers are not incentivized to pay you the lowest possible salary. They are working within restrictions the company may have set, and it's not their personal money. Keep this in mind when you negotiate, and stop treating them like your adversary.

Also, remember that while a higher paycheck is great, if your benefits are terrible, work-life balance non-existent, and you're stuck in a dead-end position, that extra cash won't make up for it. Smart candidates negotiate beyond salary.

Focusing only on salary during negotiations means you're likely missing out on significant value elsewhere. Companies typically operate within defined salary bands that limit how much they can offer in base pay, but they may have considerably more wiggle room when it comes to benefits, bonuses, and other assorted perks.

That slight salary increase you're fighting for may not really be the smartest play. Negotiating for equity, additional vacation time, or professional development opportunities can prove far more valuable in the long run. Consider that stock options at the right company could potentially multiply in value, while extra PTO directly improves your quality of life. Compensation is multidimensional, and sometimes the most valuable elements aren't found in your biweekly paycheck. Here's a great big list of all the things you can negotiate beyond salary.

Negotiable Item	Why It Matters
Signing Bonus	Companies sometimes have a budget for this, and it's an easy way to get extra cash upfront.
Performance Bonuses	Can significantly increase earnings based on results.
Stock Options & Equity	If the company grows, this can be worth way more than a salary bump. This also signifies to companies that you are thinking about being with them in the long term.
Paid Time Off (PTO)	More vacation = better work-life balance. This usually is not negotiable as it may be company policy but could be worth the conversation.
Remote Work / Flexible Hours	Priceless for avoiding burnout and commuting hell.
Professional Development Budget	Get them to pay for training, certifications, or conferences.
Relocation Assistance	Moving costs add up. Don't pay out of pocket if you don't have to.
Title Adjustments	A stronger title now = better leverage for your next job. Some companies are very strict with titles, but some will just throw around whatever title you need to make you happy.

The Worst Salary Negotiation Advice and What to Do Instead

We've already established that salary negotiation advice is everywhere, career coaches, outdated LinkedIn posts, even well-meaning family members who haven't had to negotiate a job offer in 20 years. The problem? Most of this advice is either wildly ineffective, outdated, or downright dangerous to your candidacy. If you follow the wrong negotiation strategy, you could get lowballed, ignored, or even lose the offer entirely. This section breaks down some of the worst salary negotiation myths and replaces them with real strategies that actually work.

Why Avoiding Salary Talks Until the End Can Backfire

A candidate followed the "never bring up salary first" rule, thinking it gave them an advantage. After three rounds of interviews, they finally found out the company's salary cap was $20,000 less than what they were willing to accept. They could have saved weeks of wasted time if they had clarified expectations early on.

Many job seekers deliberately postpone salary discussions until they receive an offer, believing this strategy maximizes their negotiating leverage. The thinking goes: once a company has invested time in you and wants to hire you, they'll be more willing to meet your compensation requirements. This approach can seriously backfire. Companies usually operate within defined budgets for each position, and these constraints don't suddenly disappear just because they've found their dream candidate. If your compensation expectations are significantly higher than what they've allocated for the role, delaying this conversation doesn't magically magic up additional funds that weren't in their budget for the role. Too often, it happens that candidates go through multiple interviews, investing significant time and emotional energy, only to discover at the offer stage that the compensation package falls far short of their needs.

The more effective approach is to establish a general salary range early in the process without committing to exact figures. This creates appropriate expectations on both sides while still preserving your negotiating flexibility. A simple "Based on my experience and roles I've been interviewing for, I'm looking for positions in the range of x to y but can be flexible based on other factors" can save everyone substantial time and disappointment. By addressing compensation expectations early, you ensure you're not pursuing opportunities that ultimately can't meet your financial needs, while still maintaining room to negotiate the specifics once you have a complete picture of the role and its responsibilities.

Here's some language for addressing salary early on (not first thing!): "I'm really interested in this role, and I want to make sure we're aligned on expectations. Could you share the salary range for this position?" If they press you to give a number first, say something like, "Based on my experience and what I'm seeing during my current search, I'd expect something in the $x–$y range, but I'm open to learning more about the full compensation package."

The magic word when it comes to discussing salary is *flexible*. Practice it. Repeat it. Learn to love it! The word *flexible* allows you room to ask for more later, reduces the risk of you shooting yourself in the foot by saying a number that is too high right away, and makes it clear that you plan to discuss far more than just the salary when deciding on the role.

The Danger of Asking for an Unrealistically High Number

While it's important to be reasonably assertive in negotiations, there's a real danger in pushing too far beyond reasonable expectations. Some job seekers deliberately inflate their salary requirements with the strategy that companies will simply negotiate downward to a more reasonable figure.

The reality is far more nuanced. When your ask significantly exceeds the company's range, they're likely to conclude that you're fundamentally misaligned with the position or that negotiations will be too difficult to reach a mutually acceptable agreement. Rather than engaging in extensive back-and-forth, many hiring managers will simply move on to other qualified candidates whose expectations are more aligned with their budget.

Effective negotiation isn't about requesting an arbitrarily high number—it's about understanding the market value for your skills and experience in that specific role and industry. This requires research and preparation before entering any compensation discussion.

I saw this play out firsthand with a candidate who demanded $180,000 for a position that had a firm ceiling of $140,000. Despite the candidate's qualifications, the company didn't even attempt to negotiate or counteroffer. They simply thanked the candidate for their time and proceeded with other applicants whose expectations fell within their established range. The lesson was clear: Before stating your number, understand what the market and the specific company are prepared to pay. An informed, ambitious-but-realistic request will get you much further than an unrealistically high number.

SIDEBAR

Right now, you're probably saying, "This would all be so much easier if the company just posted the salary range or told me right away what it is," and you are so right! BUT instead of adding that comment on every video I make about salary negotiations, you should write to your local government representatives and demand that salary transparency laws be enacted in your area. Seriously. But until that happens and companies are forced to do this, many of them just are not going to. So once again, I remind you, there is how we want it to be and how it is, and this is one of those how-it-is situations. I can't change it, I can only help you navigate it. Okay, back to the bad advice!

Why Saying "I'm Open to Any Salary" is a Truly Terrible Idea

Yeah, so *flexible* remains the magic word in negotiation. But don't confuse flexible with clueless. If you tell an employer, "I'm open to whatever's in the budget," they're not going to admire your adaptability. They're going to assume you are desperate for any job, and maybe you are, but remember how we already talked about how that is not actually helpful to your candidacy?

The key is to sound flexible while still setting expectations. Instead of saying, "I'm open to anything," anchor your expectations while leaving room for discussion. If they ask about your salary expectations, try, "Based on my experience and industry benchmarks, I'd expect a salary in the $x–$y range. I'd love to discuss the full compensation package to make sure it's a great fit for both of us." This approach does two things. It signals that you've done your homework. You know what's fair and what your skills are worth. It also keeps the conversation open, shows that you're willing to negotiate beyond just salary, and will consider the full compensation package (bonuses, PTO, stock, flexibility, etc.).

At the end of the day, you're not doing yourself any favors by being vague. The people who negotiate well earn more over time, get better perks, and set themselves up for stronger career moves. No one is going to hand you more money just because you seem nice. Know your value. State your expectations, and negotiate with confidence.

No, Salary Is Not Always Negotiable

Stop me if you've heard this before: *The initial offer you receive is never the company's best offer. No matter what, you should always negotiate for more.* Okay, fine. You stopped me, but I'm going to keep going. Now stop me if you've heard that from someone who has actually worked in any kind of HR or internal recruitment position within the last five years. You didn't stop me this time, did you? Good. I'm going to keep going!

To tell you the truth—and I get eaten alive on the internet every time I say this—I wish salary negotiation didn't exist. In a perfect world, there would be one salary budgeted for the role, and that salary would be paid to whoever the company hired. No higher salary bonus for being bold enough to ask, no games to get there, no paying someone less because of who they are. The salary is going to be $105,000, and that is the offer going out.

But we don't live in a perfect world, and so negotiation is a part of this process. However, I am seeing more and more companies trying to remove negotiations from the process, and usually for good reasons. Data shows that salary negotiation benefits certain people and hurts others. It is a cause of wage disparity, and it feels like playing games with people's money.

It is really important to listen to what the company is telling you. Often, they will say they don't negotiate, or the recruiter may say, "I tried to push this up, but they said the max they are going to be able to do is this amount," and they probably mean it. It is not a red flag if a company does not negotiate, and honestly, when I hear people say that they think it is a red flag, I feel bad for them. They are essentially saying that it's far more important for them to be able to play and win a silly little game than just start a relationship with their new job well.

Personally, I would rather get $100,000 and be told there is no negotiation than be given $90,000 but be able to get $100,000 if I ask for more. Sorry to the people who weren't bold enough, you get $90,000 now! Negotiating is not necessarily a sign of a flexible company. It may just be a sign of a company that built a little game into their process. Don't be put off by a company that makes a good offer then says they don't negotiate. They may have presented the best offer they can give you in order to eliminate the games.

So no, it is not true that you should *always* negotiate, especially if you are early in your career or taking a huge leap with this job.

It's Not About If You Negotiate, It's About How

You have probably heard horror stories about people who negotiated and then had an offer taken away. Unfortunately, I've had to do this in a few cases. But almost every time I've done it, it wasn't about the fact that the candidate negotiated, it was about how they negotiated. Negotiating is not a game. It's not a thing to win. It is trying to reach an agreement with people that you will hopefully be entering into a good, long-term relationship with. It is beneficial for both parties to start the role off on the right foot, and a contentious battle over a few thousand dollars is not something either side should want.

A Real Win and a Fail

Negotiation is great, in theory. Nothing drives home the stakes of a negotiation like real-world stories. The following examples illustrate the best and worst salary negotiations, and why some people double their income while others negotiate themselves out of a job.

The worst case first: I presented an offer to a candidate for $95,000, and they asked me for $110,000. I told them that is probably higher than the manager is planning to pay for the role and that maybe I could get the offer up to $100,000 or $105,000, but they were insistent that they wanted $110,000. I asked them something I always ask candidates who are having me try to get more money: "If I can get you that salary, will you accept the offer?" There is not much that is worse in negotiation than going back and trying to convince a team to pay more money, only to find out that it didn't matter anyway. The candidate said yes, that they would accept the offer in that case, so I went back and convinced the manager to convince finance to sweeten the offer and returned with the $110,000. Instead of saying yes, the candidate pushed for more and said if I could get them $115,000 and a sign-on bonus, they would take the offer today.

I warned them that this wasn't going to work. (Remember my advice about listening to what the company is telling you because they want the same thing you do?) The candidate insisted I try anyway, despite my warnings, and the hiring manager ultimately got frustrated and rescinded the offer. They told me that this person doesn't seem serious, and they were no longer interested in hiring them.

Negotiation is about balance, knowing when to push and when to accept. Pushing too hard or making it feel like a game can make a company walk away.

Here's the win. Negotiate the right way, and you can negotiate a good job offer into so much more, without even pushing too hard. This candidate received an offer for $85,000, right around what they expected. But instead of simply accepting, they asked about funding for professional development, extra PTO, and a six-month performance review with the potential for a raise. The hiring manager agreed to fund up to $3,000 for professional development, conferences, and courses, 13 days of PTO, instead of just ten, and while a company can never promise a raise (and please don't ever accept a promise of a raise), they were willing to schedule a six-month performance review rather than waiting the full year. The candidate didn't push for an unrealistic salary increase but still walked away with a significantly better deal.

Mike's take: You don't always have to push for more money. It's not all about money. Sometimes, better perks and growth opportunities are worth even more. (I will talk about this much more in the next chapter about the offer letter.) Smart, strategic negotiation gets you more without the risk of losing your offer.

Why I Turned Down A Huge Offer

A few years ago, long before I ever had TikTok, I was on the job market and thought I had found a great role. It was a small start-up, the ideal size for me. I liked the team, and it was a product I had some personal interest in, which is always helpful. I told them the salary I was targeting, and when the offer came, they hit it exactly, along with a great equity plan and 401K match. But then they sent over the benefit package and the health insurance costs, and when I say my jaw hit the floor, I mean MY. JAW. HIT. THE. FLOOR. I had never seen such high benefit costs in my life. They didn't even have a family plan. You had to pay the full cost for each person on your insurance plan, which is a huge nightmare for parents of multiple children. All in all, the premium costs for the worst benefit plan with a huge deductible would have cost me about $25,000 a year, before spending any actual money on the deductible!

I immediately declined the offer and told them exactly why. Truth be told, I was disappointed in myself for not asking about these costs earlier in the process, but I never anticipated that they would be that high. Lesson learned, I always ask now. Maybe the company thought that I was playing hardball. They quickly countered, offering an additional $20,000 to the salary, which would have offset a lot of the benefits costs and would have been more money than I had ever made. But the more I thought about it, the clearer it became that I'd still be paying $5,000 out of pocket just to have benefits, plus the huge deductible I'd be responsible for, plus the fact that insurance costs rise every year, aaaaaaand the fact that as a recruiter, I'd be the person sending these offers to candidates in the future and pretending they weren't awful. I said no.

It is important to understand that while a higher salary pays the bills, it isn't everything. Total compensation matters just as much, if not more. A higher salary does not always mean you are in the best position you could be. I always warn people not to get locked into a set salary number you have to hit but rather focus on the entire picture. $100,000 with fully covered benefits is a much higher compensation plan for most people than $110,000 with standard benefits. That is why I preach over and over again that *flexibility* is the magic word.

How to Get the Top of the Range

If you've been paying attention up to this point, you've probably noticed that my negotiation advice differs from a lot of people's. This is because, as a recruiter, I focus on speaking honestly and openly during negotiations. If you do this my way, you agreed in the first interview about an expected salary range and also made it clear that you also care about things like benefits costs, finding the right job, and did not present the company with any surprises at the end.

More often than not, if you do it this way, the offer you receive is exactly where you'd expect or within a reasonable range to get it there. I have seen many more people be successful by being clear about what they want up front than I have seen people do well by being secretive and aloof. This is because salary negotiation does not start when you get an offer; it starts with the first contact you make with the company, even in the application stage. People always ask me how to get an offer at the top of the range. And while it's not always possible, here is what people who get top-of-the-range offers do:

- Submit a strong application and resume, including great answers to any application questions.
- Communicate quickly and clearly throughout the whole process.
- Discuss salary early in the process and ask the company questions about how they make salary decisions within the range.
- Perform exceptionally on all interviews and assignments throughout the process.
- Ask if there is flexibility to get to the top of the range when presented with the verbal offer or in order to understand why they were not offered the top of the range, based on earlier conversations.

If you're reaching out to ask me how to negotiate a maximum salary offer once the offer is already in hand, it's probably too late. This is one of the big things people fail to realize when it comes to salary negotiations: you have been negotiating from the very beginning, and the company has been paying attention.

The people who tell you never to say a number, to keep your cards hidden, and give other advice that comes from a place of contention rather than cooperation have not successfully negotiated any offers recently. I'm willing to say pretty confidently that I know who most of these people are, and they haven't gotten a job or worked in a hiring capacity in many many years. They don't have your best interests at heart. They just are saying what you want to hear, and when it doesn't work, they won't be anywhere to be found, and it won't matter to them that their bad advice hurt you. I do not excuse myself from this criticism of career gurus either. As much as I want you to be successful, if you aren't, nothing bad will happen to me. I have zero stakes in your success outside of the nice DM you may send me when you are successful. That is a big reason why I warned you at the start of this chapter to take only the advice you are comfortable with or find beneficial. None of us gurus is drawing you a precise treasure map to follow.

The bottom line is that negotiation is not a battle between adversaries. Ideally, it's two parties working to establish the terms of their relationship to get off on the right foot. Negotiation isn't just about money. Things like benefit costs can swing your total comp by thousands. Perks can be even more valuable. How you negotiate is far more important than if. And sometimes there really isn't wiggle room. Listen to what the company is telling you. The company started negotiations the second you applied. Catch up!

Why Counteroffers Are Often a Trap

You've done it. You landed an offer at another company, and now your current employer suddenly realizes you exist. Out of nowhere, they want to talk. They're offering more money, better perks, maybe even the promotion they swore "was coming soon." It's tempting. Why leave if you can get what you want *without* having to start fresh?

Here's the problem: Most counteroffers are a trap. Companies don't give counteroffers because they suddenly see your worth. They give them because they hate losing, and because it's easier and cheaper to keep you than to replace you. And if you accept, you might feel like a winner in the short term, but the long-term consequences could be worse than you expect.

Most counteroffers are nothing more than a temporary Band-Aid on a long-term problem. Hiring is expensive, training new employees is a hassle, and unexpected turnover makes leadership look bad. So when an employee walks in with an external offer, suddenly, they're valued just enough to warrant a last-minute raise or a half-hearted promise of change.

But here's the truth: If your company truly valued you, they wouldn't need an ultimatum to pay you what you're worth. If they suddenly have the budget to match your external offer, ask yourself: Why didn't they give you that raise before you were halfway out the door? The reality is that most counteroffers are reactive, not proactive. They aren't a genuine investment in you—they're an emergency measure to plug a hole in their team and avoid dealing with a messy hiring process.

Even if the extra money feels like a win, counteroffers rarely fix the reasons you were looking for a new job in the first place. A toxic work environment doesn't magically become healthy just because your paycheck is bigger. That micromanaging boss? Still there. That lack of career growth? Still a problem. That crushing workload? Probably worse now because that raise is coming with management's expectation that you will be working even harder.

On top of that, once you take their counteroffer, you've changed the dynamic at your job forever. You're likely no longer seen as a long-term fit at the company but rather a hired gun they threw money at because they weren't prepared to lose you. But they'll be ready next time you get an offer. In fact, they're probably already preparing for it now. You'll feel the relationships and workplace shift around you, and not for the better.

This is why most people who accept counteroffers still leave within a year. They are often debated, but there are studies that show that most employees who take a counteroffer end up resigning within 12 months anyway, not because they suddenly found a better opportunity but because the same frustrations that drove them to look elsewhere were never really resolved.

I have worked with countless candidates who landed an offer only to be wooed back by a counteroffer of more money and, of course, a promise to fix the things that were the problem to begin with. It always seems like an easy win, the same job, same colleagues, just more money. But so often, they realize nothing else has changed. Their problems are all still there: their stagnant career trajectory, the lack of leadership support, the same frustrating roadblocks. I have had so many calls with candidates six months later who want to know if the job is still available, and it never is.

The takeaway? A counteroffer might solve your short-term money problem, but it won't solve your long-term career problem. If your company only sees your value when you're walking out the door, that should tell you everything you need to know.

When a Counteroffer *Might* Be Worth Considering

While counteroffers come with significant risks, there are select situations where they might genuinely deserve your consideration. Conventional wisdom warns against accepting them, but certain circumstances can justify real consideration.

Maybe you really were just leaving for a higher paycheck, and you're totally fine with nothing else changing at your job, except for a boss who trusts you a little bit less, as long as your paycheck is higher. If money was truly your only consideration, and you are otherwise happy, you can go ahead and consider that counteroffer.

A counteroffer also becomes more viable when it includes substantial career advancement opportunities beyond just increased compensation. Suppose your current employer offers you not only more money but also expanded responsibilities, a meaningful title change, or access to projects that align with your long-term career goals. In that case, these elements add legitimate value to their proposition and probably signify a chance to stay for the long term. It's unlikely they would promote you into a new role just to let you go shortly after.

Context matters. If your company had already been in discussions about your advancement before you received an outside offer, their counteroffer may represent an acceleration of plans already in motion rather than a desperate retention tactic. This suggests the company had already recognized your value and was planning to invest in your growth.

Even in these scenarios, proceed with caution. The statistics that show high departure rates after accepting a counteroffer are real, and the fundamental issues that initially drove you to look elsewhere may remain unresolved beneath a temporary financial fix.

The Right Way to Navigate a Counteroffer Conversation

If you're going to entertain a counteroffer, do it with a clear head and a solid plan. The worst thing you can do is get swept up in the moment, accept more money, and assume things will magically improve. If you're staying, make sure it's because the job itself is getting better, not just for the bigger paycheck. A raise is great, but if your role, responsibilities, or career trajectory aren't changing, you're just getting paid slightly more to tolerate the same problems while starting a potential timer on your employment there.

Be direct about what you want. If the reason you were job-searching was lack of growth, lack of flexibility, or a toxic work culture, money alone won't fix that. If you're considering staying, be specific in what you're asking for. Are they offering an actual promotion with new responsibilities and career development? Are they giving you a defined path forward, or just hoping the extra cash will make you stop looking?

And whatever they promise, get it in writing. If they tell you a promotion is "in the works" or that they'll "revisit things in six months," assume that means never. Promotions that aren't documented in a formal offer or contract tend to conveniently disappear once the threat of you leaving is off the table. If they truly want to invest in your future, they'll be happy to put it in writing.

Most importantly, don't use an external offer as leverage unless you're really willing to walk. Too many candidates assume that threatening to leave will guarantee them a raise, but it can easily backfire. If leadership sees you as disloyal or a flight risk, they may give you the raise today even as they start looking for your replacement tomorrow.

A counteroffer should never be a quick fix to avoid change. If you're staying, stay because the role is evolving in ways that genuinely benefit you and your career, not just because they threw some extra money your way. Otherwise, you'll likely be right back on the job market within a year, wondering why you didn't leave when you had the chance.

Here are ways to respond to a counteroffer:

If you're not interested in staying: "Thanks for the offer, but I've already made my decision. I appreciate everything I've learned here, but I'm excited for this new opportunity."
If you're considering it but need more info: "I appreciate the offer. Can we talk more about long-term growth and what role adjustments would look like? I want to make sure this decision is best for both of us."
If you're torn and need time:"This is a big decision, and I want to make sure I'm thinking everything through carefully. Can I have 24–48 hours to consider this?"

A Real World Win That Failed

One of the first declined offers of my career came from a candidate I'll call Justin. I got him a job offer at a huge local company with a $15,000 salary increase and a leadership title. It turned out that Justin was really only job searching for leverage to get a raise at his current company. It worked, and he got a $15,000 bump and declined the offer I had made him, and rather rudely, I must say.

But here's what happened next: Justin's manager started treating him differently, knowing he had been looking elsewhere. When layoffs came a few months later, he was among the first to be let go. The company that had offered him the job? That role had already been filled, of course.

Mike's take: Using an outside offer as leverage can work. But it also can put a target on your back. I don't tell this story as some kind of warning never to try it but to make sure that you understand that there is a lot of risk involved.

The bottom line is that most counteroffers are made because it's better for the company to keep you than to start looking for a new hire, not because they suddenly value you more. If you aren't planning to take a counteroffer, be very direct. Don't waffle and debate over it. Rip off the Band-aid. The best counteroffers come with real career growth, not just more money. If you do accept, get everything in writing. Verbal promises mean nothing.

At the end of the day, your career growth shouldn't depend on ultimatums. If a company only values you when you have another offer, that tells you everything you need to know. Make sure that whatever decision you make is based on long-term success, not short-term convenience.

Wrapping Up Your Negotiation Strategy – How to Get What You Deserve (Without Losing the Offer)

By now, you know that negotiation isn't about squeezing out a few extra bucks; it's about crafting the best overall compensation package for your long-term career growth. But a strong negotiation strategy isn't just about the numbers; it's also about how you approach the conversation from the start, how you frame your asks, and—most importantly—knowing when to push and when to accept a great offer.

This section wraps up the biggest lessons from this chapter, ensuring you have a clear, actionable negotiation mindset that will serve you well for every job offer to come.

After successfully negotiating a strong offer, properly handling the final steps is crucial.

First, ensure everything discussed is documented in writing. If the company promised conditional benefits like a six-month performance review with a potential raise or future stock grants, make sure these commitments appear in your formal offer letter or employment contract.

Continue to behave professionally throughout this process. Even if negotiations were challenging or contentious at times, conclude the process on a positive note that sets the stage for a productive working relationship. Even if you ultimately decide to decline an offer, do so respectfully and graciously. The professional world is remarkably interconnected, and relationships have a way of circling back unexpectedly. The hiring manager you impress with your professionalism today might become a valuable connection tomorrow.

Example of a Strong Offer Acceptance Email:

> **Subject:** Excited to join [Company Name] – offer acceptance
>
> Hi [hiring manager's name],
>
> I'm thrilled to accept the offer for the [job title] position at [Company Name]! I truly appreciate the opportunity and the time the team has spent discussing how I can contribute to [specific project or goal].
> I've reviewed the offer details, and everything looks great. Please let me know if there are any next steps or paperwork I should complete. I'm excited to get started on [start date] and looking forward to joining the team!
> Best,
> [Your Name]

Mike's Snarky Do's and Don'ts of Negotiation

DO start proving your worth at first contact. Your application and emails are part of the negotiation.

DO make your ask about total compensation. Salary, stock, PTO, bonuses—it all matters.

DO approach negotiation as a conversation, not a confrontation. Be confident, not aggressive.

DO keep your emotions in check. It's business, not personal.

DO accept or decline gracefully. Your reputation follows you.

DON'T negotiate just for the sake of it. If the offer is great, don't risk it by testing limits.

DON'T ignore benefits and perks. Sometimes, more PTO or stock is worth more than a salary bump.

DON'T accept a counteroffer without thinking it through. If they only gave you a raise when you threatened to leave, that's a red flag.

DON'T make negotiation a game. If you keep pushing beyond reason, companies will move on.

At the end of the day, negotiation isn't about "winning." It's about making sure you're set up for success in this job and the next one. Companies expect negotiation, but they also expect professionalism. Know your worth, make the right moves, and leave the negotiation table with a better deal and a strong reputation.

CHAPTER TEN

Decoding the Offer Letter

TL;DR

Your offer letter is not just a formality. It's a legally binding contract that could make or break your career. If you don't read it carefully, you might end up with less money, fewer rights, and more legal restrictions than you expected. Take your time, ask questions, and make sure you're signing a deal you actually want, not just the one they hope you won't notice.

This chapter is not exciting, but it is important. I've included a full checklist at the end. Take the time to read through this as you get closer to offer time.

Understanding the Offer Letter as a Contract

Your job search doesn't end when you get an offer. It should be a moment of relief, but let's not pop the champagne just yet. That offer letter? It's a contract, and like any contract, it's been crafted to protect the company, not you. This is where too many candidates trip up. They skim the offer, see the number they expected (or close enough), sign on the dotted line, and get blindsided later when their first paycheck doesn't look quite right, their "bonus" mysteriously vanishes, or they find out they accidentally agreed to a noncompete that could torpedo their future job prospects.

Mistakes here are costly. The excitement of a job offer can cloud your judgment and make it easy to assume everything is exactly as it was discussed in the interview process. Bad news: If it's not written in that offer letter, it doesn't exist. Whatever the recruiter told you? It's not real unless it's on paper. That "performance-based bonus" they hyped up? If there's no mention of how it's calculated, assume it's as real as a unicorn. And if you think companies always "do the right thing" when things aren't explicitly spelled out, I have a bridge to sell you.

An offer letter is a legal document, and you need to treat it like one. That means slowing down, reading the fine print, and understanding that there's more to this than just your base salary. You don't need a law degree to get through it, but you do need to approach it with the same scrutiny you'd give any major financial decision. Would you sign a mortgage without understanding the interest rate? Would you agree to a car lease without knowing the monthly payments? Would you agree to Apple's Terms and Conditions without reading them first? Okay, fine. That one was a joke. Of course you would! But don't do that with your offer letter.

The Biggest Offer Letter Mistakes People Make

They sign too quickly. You're excited. You want to say yes. Maybe you're worried they'll rescind the offer if you take too long. Pro tip: They won't as long as you are communicative. Rushing leads to regret. Take your time.

They believe verbal promises. If it's not in writing, it's not real. Period. Your recruiter may be wonderful, but they don't control payroll, and they won't be able to fight for you six months down the line when that promised increase doesn't come.

They ignore vague language. "Bonus potential" is a term designed to make you feel good that means nothing.

They overlook legal clauses. Noncompetes, clawback agreements, and IP ownership clauses can all have long-term consequences. You need to know what they actually mean before you sign.

They don't ask for clarification. You're not being difficult by asking questions. You are being smart. If something isn't clear, ask. If they dodge the question? That's your answer.

SIDEBAR

This chapter is going to sound awfully negative. You are going to hear some horror stories because I want to make my points, but I also want to say that I don't believe most managers or recruiters operate with ill intent. Everything I said in the last chapter about being on the same team is still true, so don't read this chapter and decide to start a fight over language in your offer letter. That said, legal terms are meant to give the company an out, and anything that is not in writing on the document that you sign, legally, was never actually promised to you. While these documents are written to benefit the company, it does not mean that anyone is actively trying to screw you over. I just want you to be aware of all of this so you know to ask the right questions and see how you feel about the answers.

Compensation and Benefits: What's Really in Your Paycheck?

Just as I discussed in the last chapter about negotiation, if you are only focused on your base salary, you are setting yourself up to be let down. Base salary is the flashy number they dangle in front of you, but it's not what actually ends up in your bank account. The reality is that total compensation is a puzzle made up of salary, bonuses, benefits, stock, and perks—or in some cases, a minefield filled with hidden costs that eat into your paycheck faster than you can say "direct deposit." (Note that I talk about each of these briefly and in more depth later on in the chapter.)

Most job seekers fixate on that bolded number on their offer letter. It's the easiest thing to compare, right? But if you only focus on base pay and ignore the fine print, you could end up making less money overall, even with a higher salary. I've seen people turn down jobs that had better retirement benefits, stock options, and PTO just because the base salary was a few thousand dollars less than their other option. Or worse, terrible health insurance costs that will derail your lifestyle. (Remember my personal example in the last chapter?) Don't be that person. You need to think bigger.

First, let's break down the myth of **base salary**. That $100,000 offer? It might actually be $90,000 after you realize $10,000 of it is tied up in a "performance-based" bonus that may or may not ever materialize. And even if it does, it could be taxed at a higher rate than your salary, meaning you'll see less of it anyway. Or maybe your $120,000 offer includes a one-time $15,000 signing bonus—nice for year one, but suddenly you're making $105,000 after that. Some companies love playing these little tricks because they know candidates get starry-eyed over big numbers and don't do the math.

Speaking of illusions, let's talk about **stock options**. Stock options are the part of offer letters that people tend to understand the least. "We offer generous equity," they say. Or they throw a random number of options at you, which really means nothing to you at this point. Or they may give you the amount that it is "worth," the equivalent of $150,000 in stock options." The truth is that equity is sort of just made-up money that most people will never see. It's also really important to know the difference between stock grants and RSUs, which I'll get into a bit later. I'm a startup guy. I've worked for quite a few of them, and I've been given all kinds of "generous equity packages" as part of signing, but I've never collected a single penny. Equity can be a great add-on to an offer, but don't let yourself be fooled into taking less money than you need because there was a promise of equity.

It is also so easy to ignore your **401(k)**. I'm very guilty of this myself, but if you are not taking advantage of this benefit, you are literally passing up free money. There is a huge difference between a company that offers a 0% match, a 2% match, and a 7–10% match. (It's rare but I've seen it!) I'm not here to talk to you about saving for retirement, or market conditions, or any of that because it's all a different language to me. BUT, if you are making $100,000 per year and putting 5% of it into your 401(k) along with a 5% match from your company, you are essentially getting a $5,000 pre-tax bonus every single year. Maybe this is not the sexiest perk to you, but it is a perk nonetheless, and it is one that will continue to build on itself the longer you take advantage. Don't ignore this!

Bonuses and commissions are another area where candidates can end up being let down. Discretionary bonuses? That's a fancy way of saying you might get it, but you also might not. And commission-based roles? Companies will throw out theoretical max earnings (called OTE or On Target Earnings) to make the offer sound sexier. Still, then you need to ask: What do average performers actually make? How many people on the team hit the target last year? If they're dangling a number no one ever hits, that's not real money. I can tell you my sales role has a $600K OTE, but if the reality is you're only going to hit 40% of that target, then you won't be making anywhere close to that max earnings number. I'll have more to say about bonuses in a bit.

Then there's the silent killer of compensation: **benefits**, or lack thereof. A bad benefits package can drain your salary faster than my FanDuel addiction. (I'm kidding, Karen. I always bet modestly!) If you're paying $600 monthly for health insurance, have zero employer 401(k) match, and barely any PTO, you're effectively making thousands less than you think. In contrast, a job that pays a little less but has fully covered healthcare, a generous retirement plan, and extra PTO could be worth far more in the long run.

Let's break this down. Say you get two job offers. One is for $100,000 with free healthcare and a 5% 401(k) match. The other is for $110,000, but you're paying $500/month for insurance, and there's no 401(k) match. When you factor in those costs, the $100,000 job is actually worth more. But most candidates don't think this way. They see a bigger number and assume it's better. Don't be most candidates!

So, what's the move? Before signing anything, run the total compensation check. Look beyond base salary and factor in bonuses, stock, insurance costs, retirement contributions, and PTO. If something isn't clear, ask. If a company is dodgy about answering, assume it's bad news. And if your recruiter keeps saying, "I'll check on that and get back to you," make sure they actually do.

A Real World Story

I had a client who thought she was getting a $120,000 job, a base salary of $110,000 plus a $10,000"performance-based" bonus. That's what the recruiter told her. Sounds great, right?

Payday came. No bonus. She checked her offer letter. Guess what? The bonus was never actually guaranteed. The company only paid it once per year, if they hit revenue targets and only to employees rated as "high performers," whatever that meant. Spoiler: They didn't hit revenue targets. She didn't get the bonus.

Mike's take: If a bonus isn't clearly defined in your offer letter—how it's calculated, when it's paid, and what conditions apply—don't count that money as part of your income. It may still come. I don't think that, in this case, they told my client about a bonus with zero intent to pay it, but a performance bonus is ultimately a discretionary bonus, so you can't just assume it will show up in your bank account. Recruiters and managers love to *hype up* bonuses because they make offers sound better. But unless the details are in writing, it's just wishful thinking.

Don't get distracted by salary alone. The difference between a great job and a financial disaster isn't just how much you make but how much you keep. Do the math. Read the fine print. And for the love of God, stop assuming that thing you're concerned about probably won't matter.

Discretionary Bonuses, Stock Options, and Other "Maybe" Money

You know that moment when you get a job offer and they throw in a "performance-based" bonus or some "generous stock options," and you immediately start calculating what kind of car you'll buy with all that extra cash? Yeah. Stop. Right. There. Because unless you read the fine print, that bonus might never hit your account, and those stock options could be about as valuable as Monopoly money.

Discretionary Bonuses

I've already touched on this a few times, but let's really dig into the classic trap of discretionary bonuses. The word "discretionary" is doing a lot of heavy lifting here. It means the company can choose whether to pay you that bonus. And guess what? When budgets get tight— they almost always do—that bonus is often the first thing to disappear. Most bonuses are broken into a 50/50 structure where 50% is based on your performance, and 50% is based on the company's performance. This means that even if you smash every one of your goals, the company can still get away with only giving you 50% of your bonus. You'll be sitting at your desk in December, waiting for that nice holiday payout, and instead, you get an email about "challenging business conditions" and how they "appreciate your hard work." No check, just vibes. It may feel tough to ask, but you're allowed to ask about the actual payout history. Have they given out the full amount before, or is this some mythical number that only exists in the CFO's fantasy world?

Let me be clear. I'm not saying you should decline a bonus as part of your comp. Bonuses can be great extra income for many people. But if you gave me the choice of a higher base salary or a discretionary bonus, I'd taking the salary every time.

Stock Options vs. RSUs (Restricted Stock Units)

Now let's get into stock options versus RSUs because this is where a lot of people start imagining themselves as future millionaires when in reality, they might not even be able to afford the buy-in. Stock options mean you have the option, not the guarantee, to buy company stock at a set price (strike price). The way options typically work is on a four-year vesting period with a one-year cliff. In non-corporate-speak, this means that on your one-year anniversary at the company, you'll gain access to purchase 25% of the options that were in your offer letter. You don't have to purchase them now. Most people don't, but that is when you get access to them. Every month for the next 36 months, you then get access to 1/36 of the remaining options. So what it would typically look like is this:

- 10,000 stock options are given to you in the offer letter with a strike price of what the company estimates the equity would be worth today on the market. (Though if they are not a public company, it's still technically worth $0.) The earlier you get into a company, the lower this price is, which is good, but the longer it will be until the equity is worth real money.

- At the one-year mark, you get access to 2,500 options. Every month after that, you get 1/36 of the remaining options.
- On your fourth anniversary, you gain access to purchase all 10,000 options at the original strike price you were given, which should (in theory) be much lower than the current strike price four years later.

That sounds great when the company's value is skyrocketing, and you were there from the start, but what happens when the stock is worth less than your strike price because it turns out you weren't working for the next Google? Nothing. You don't exercise them, and they expire. Poof. Gone. Or if you get laid off 11 months in, guess what you get? Nothing at all because you never vested in any options. When you are vested in options and leave the company, an expiration date is also attached to those options, meaning you need to make a purchase decision sooner than you'd like.

For example, let's stay with the above scenario, and you leave or are laid off two years into your contract. You have vested in 5,000 options, but now there is a date by which you have to exercise them. When you work for the company, you don't have to worry about this, but now that you are no longer with them, your options are now use-them-or-lose-them. The company may be three years away from going public and assigning any real value to those options, but you have to decide now whether you want to exercise those 5,000 options at the strike price and hope for the best or just let them go. If you do exercise them, you're shelling out your own cash to buy shares that you hope will be worth more someday. Even at a low strike price like $2 per share, that is still $10,000 you have to invest into a company that just laid you off in hopes that it may be worth more in a few years.

Again, there is nothing wrong with equity. Some people have struck gold with it, but that is not the normal case. Don't run from equity-heavy companies, but understand what you will be making in real money versus what you are making in what may wind up being magical fairy money.

RSUs (restricted stock units), on the other hand, are actual shares given to you over time. You don't have to buy them. They just vest, meaning they gradually become yours as long as you stay with the company. This is real compensation, but even here, there's a catch: vesting schedules. If your RSUs vest over four years and you leave after two? Congrats, you're walking away with half (or less) of what they promised. And taxes? You're being given real value equity every month. Uncle Sam will take a piece of that as well.

Here's the truth: Less than 10% of startups actually go public or get acquired at a meaningful valuation. That means your stock could be completely worthless. And even if the company does survive, how do you cash out? Are they publicly traded? Can you sell your shares or do you have to hold onto them and wait for a miracle? If they're offering equity, that's great. But it is not a replacement for your compensation, and for most of you, it won't ever pay your bills.

Let's talk about how companies inflate total compensation with these "maybe" earnings. You see a job posting that says, "Total Comp: $180,000." Wow, right? But when you break it down, base salary is $110,000, stock options make up $50,000, and the remaining $20,000 is a bonus that you may or may not ever see. That means only $110,000 is guaranteed money. The rest is just a fancy way to make the offer look better than it is. So, before you start picturing yourself rolling in cash, ask yourself one question: If the market crashes, the company underperforms, or you leave early, how much of this compensation will you actually see? If the answer isn't "all of it," then you're taking on all the risk.

Before you sign anything, get clear answers. Is the bonus guaranteed? What's the company's track record on paying it out? Are the stock options actually worth anything? Or are you getting shares in a company that will be out of business in 18 months? How much of your pay is locked behind "maybes" and "ifs" instead of cash you can count on? Because at the end of the day, if you can't put it in your bank account, it's not real money.

A Real-World Story

Sarah was pumped. After months of job searching, she finally landed a great offer, with a $15,000 signing bonus. She signed immediately, barely glancing at the fine print. A few weeks in, she decided to actually read the offer letter—a little late, but better than never. That's when she saw it: a clawback clause. If she left before she'd been there 18 months, she'd have to pay back every dollar of that signing bonus. Annoying, but not uncommon. Then she dug deeper. The kicker? If she got laid off, she still had to return the money. Even if the company let her go for reasons completely out of her control, they could just deduct the $15,000 straight from her final paycheck. Fast-forward a year, and Sarah had a new offer from a company that reached out and recruited her. It was a $15,000 increase, but she was also going to have to pay her company back $15,000 when she left, which not only negated the increase in her first year but also left her having to pay that money up front, before even earning it in the new role. Sarah was able to ask her new company for a sign-on bonus to help cover some of this money in case she had to pay it back. She also made sure that she would not have to pay back that sign-on bonus if she left. But not everybody is so fortunate.

Mike's take: Signing bonuses aren't always free money. If there's a clawback clause, ask how long do you have to stay before you don't owe anything. What happens if you're laid off? Will they deduct it from your final paycheck, or can you pay over time?

Other Hidden Legal Clauses That Can Trap You

Your offer letter might look like an innocent little contract, just a few pages confirming your salary, start date, and title, but there could also be a legal trap hidden in the fine print that could haunt you long after you've left the company. These clauses aren't just words; they're handcuffs disguised as paperwork. If you don't read carefully, you could be signing away your right to work in your own industry, handing over ownership of your side projects, or even committing to paying back your signing bonus just for daring to leave before an arbitrary deadline.

Let's start with **noncompete agreements**, one of corporate America's favorite ways to keep you stuck. A noncompete is a clause that says you can't work for a competitor or start your own competing business for a set period of time after leaving. Sounds straightforward until you realize that some companies define "competitor" as any business remotely related to what they do, which means you could be barred from working anywhere in your industry for months or even years. Some states, like California, have banned noncompetes outright, but companies still try to sneak them in, hoping you won't challenge them. There are currently ongoing legal battles over noncompetes on a national level, but for now, even in states where enforcement is weak, employers use them as scare tactics because most people won't risk a lawsuit just to change jobs and tend to be intimidated by legal issues they don't understand.

Then we have **clawback clauses**, the hidden landmines that not only effect signing bonuses, but also relocation packages, and even stock grants. A clawback clause means that if you leave before a certain period, the company can demand you pay back all or part of the money they gave you upfront. That $20,000 signing bonus? If you leave six months in, you might need to repay it all. And some contracts don't just claw back the cash, they can even deduct it from your final paycheck without asking. If you think this is rare, think again. Companies love using clawbacks to keep employees from leaving, dangling a fat bonus in front of you, then effectively making you "pay" for it if you dare to leave before they say you can.

Now let's talk about **intellectual property (IP) and confidentiality agreements**, which can extend far beyond your actual job. Some companies write contracts that go so far as to claim that anything you create while employed, whether on company time or not, belongs to them. That means if you're a software engineer who codes an app on weekends, an artist who sells paintings online, or even someone running a niche TikTok account, your employer might legally claim ownership over your work. And they will enforce it if they think there's money to be made.

The real kicker? Many offer letters don't spell these clauses out clearly. They bury them in legal jargon, assuming you won't dig deep enough to notice. That's why you need to read every word and ask questions before signing. If an employer refuses to clarify or won't budge on restrictive clauses, that's a massive red flag.

Your salary and benefits won't matter if you're locked into a contract that controls your career. If an employer tries to rush you into signing without giving you time to review the legal terms, that's not a mistake—it's a strategy. Take the time to read, ask questions, and if something feels off, get a lawyer to look at it. Because once you sign, you've agreed to play by their rules.

A Real World Story

A friend of mine took a role at a tech company a few years back. The salary was solid, benefits looked good, and he was about to sign. But something felt off about the noncompete clause that seemed like it would have blocked him from working in his industry for two years if he ever quit. When my friend asked about it, HR brushed it off: *"Oh, we never actually enforce those."* Here's the thing. My friend's wife had just been through her own version of this. She had also been told that "we never enforce those." But they actually did enforce it and scared a new company off from hiring her.

In his case, my friend pushed back and negotiated the clause out entirely. If they never enforce it, they should be willing to remove it, right? A year later, he got an even better offer, and because he wasn't legally locked out, he took it. No issues.

Mike's take: Noncompetes are a tricky thing, and I'm not a lawyer, so I can't give legal advice. Even as I write, there are cases in the courts over the legality of noncompete clauses, so I don't know what to tell you about them in general. But, I do feel comfortable saying taking a company's promise of "don't worry about it" is not usually a great idea. Some noncompetes are not legal and can't be enforced. Others are enforced through intimidation, like in the case of my friend's wife. The best advice I can give is to read everything. And if it looks sketchy, get legal advice.

SHOULD YOU CONSULT AN EMPLOYMENT LAWYER?

If you think employment lawyers are only for people getting sued or fired, think again. The best time to call one is before you need one. Your employer had lawyers draft your contract to protect them, so why shouldn't you have someone make sure it also protects you? Trust me, if there's a legal loophole that benefits the company, that's where it will be.

Let's start with when you need a lawyer. If your contract has a noncompete that could block you from working in your industry for a year, a clawback clause that demands you pay back your signing bonus if you leave, or an IP agreement that claims they own your personal work, it's time to bring in a pro. Even if you don't see anything obviously concerning, contracts are full of vague legal language designed to sound harmless but that can completely screw you over later. And if you find yourself thinking, *"This is just standard legal stuff,"* congratulations, you've fallen for it, exactly what they want.

People assume you can only negotiate salary and bonuses, but you can and should push back on legal terms too. Noncompetes? Many companies will soften or remove them if challenged. Clawbacks? You can ask to shorten the payback period or reduce the amount you owe if you leave early. Intellectual property clauses? Get in writing that your side hustles belong to you. Employers don't advertise that these things are negotiable, but they absolutely can be, especially if they want you.

If you've already signed a bad contract, don't panic. First, check if the clause is actually enforceable. If you're hit with a clawback demand, a lawyer might be able to negotiate a reduced repayment or get it waived entirely. And if you're leaving a job where your contract claims they own everything you create, a lawyer can help determine if that holds up legally.

The Bottom Line:

If you answer yes to any of these questions, get a professional legal opinion before signing:

- Is there a noncompete that limits your career?
- Do you have to pay back bonuses, stock, or relocation money?
- Does the contract say the company owns your personal projects?
- Is the contract full of legal jargon that makes no sense to you, a human who may not have gone to law school?
- Are you in a high-stakes industry like tech, finance, or startups where contracts are more complex?

Final Offer Review Checklist

Congratulations, you made it to the final step, signing your offer letter. But slow down before you go grab that pen and declare victory. Your offer letter is a legally binding contract, and once you sign, you're locked in. And if you didn't read it carefully? Well, that's how people can end up in career jail, stuck in jobs where they're underpaid, overworked, and legally screwed if they try to leave.

Excitement makes people rush this part. You got the offer, and now you just want to make it official. But smart job seekers know that this is a time to pump the brakes, not hit the gas. Remember, if the recruiter said one thing and the letter says another, assume the letter is correct. So rushing through the paperwork because you "trust the company" or "don't want to cause trouble" is exactly how people sign away their flexibility, their financial future, and in some cases, their right to work in their own industry. So, take a deep breath, get some coffee, and let's go over this offer because if something is missing, unclear, or just doesn't sit right, you need to address it before signing, not after. Lucky for you, I made this handy-dandy list to help you through this part.

Make sure the offer reflects what you actually discussed.

- Do the job title and responsibilities match what was described and discussed?
- Is there any vague language that could allow them to change your role or compensation later?

Compensation Clarity

- Is your base salary exactly what was promised?
- Are bonuses clearly defined, or are they "discretionary" (really, wishful thinking)?
- Is your stock grant actually valuable, or will it take four years of indentured servitude before you see a dime? Are they stock options you need to purchase later, or will you be given RSUs?

- Are your benefits saving you money, or will high insurance premiums eat up your raise?

Benefits Breakdown

- Do you know what your healthcare plan covers?
- What will your out-of-pocket costs be?
- Do you fully understand the 401(k) match?
- Is your PTO spelled out clearly, including how it accrues?

PTO & Work Flex

- Do they list the exact number of vacation days and how you earn them, or is it "unlimited PTO"? If the latter, which can be good or bad, make sure you have clarity around the expectations and average amount of time people take off. If they won't clarify, assume the worst.
- What is their policy regarding work flexibility? Is it a lot of talk or is it real?

Legal Restrictions. Spot these now.

Companies throw these things into contracts assuming most people won't question them, but if you do question them, they'll often adjust things to keep you on board.

- Is there a noncompete that bans you from working in your field for years? If a noncompete is overly broad, you can ask them to change it.
- Is there a clawback clause that could force you to pay back your signing bonus if you leave early? (This is common and not necessarily a red flag, but if it's there, you should at least know about it. If a clawback is too aggressive, ask for a shorter payback period, 12 months instead of the original 18 in the offer.
- Does the company claim ownership over anything you create, even outside of work? If an IP clause claims own-

ership over your personal projects, have it rewritten to exclude work you do on your own time.

Get a second opinion.

Employment lawyers exist for a reason, and a quick review could save you from years of regret. If a company pressures you to "sign immediately" or acts offended that you want to review the fine print, that's a massive red flag. Any company that respects its employees will respect your right to review the contract. If they don't, what does that tell you about how they treat people once they're locked in?

Read. Everything. Twice. Your offer letter isn't a formality—it's the last hurdle before committing to an employer. Slow down. Read everything. If something looks off, ask about it. Negotiate if needed. And if you have any doubts? Get a second opinion, whether it's from a mentor, a lawyer, or just someone who's been through this before. Because once you sign, you're locked in, and all the "But my recruiter said..." excuses in the world won't change what's on that paper.

Signing an offer letter isn't about making the employer happy; it's about protecting yourself. You're not just agreeing to work there. You're agreeing to their rules. So make sure those rules work for you. Because once that ink dries, you're stuck with them.

Mike's Great You-Got-the-Offer-in-Writing Do's and Don'ts

DO read everything. Twice. If it's written down, it matters. If it's not, make them write it.

DO confirm your total compensation. Is the salary what you expected? Are bonuses guaranteed or just fairy dust?

DO scrutinize legal clauses. Noncompetes, clawbacks, and intellectual property agreements could screw you over later.

DO negotiate. If they refuse to clarify or adjust unreasonable terms, consider that your first red flag.

DO take your time. No legitimate company will punish you for reading before signing. If they do, run.

DO get a second opinion. A mentor, career coach, or employment lawyer can save you from years of regret.

DON'T rush to sign. This is not an iTunes Terms & Conditions agreement. You actually need to read this one.

DON'T trust verbal promises. If they say, "Oh, don't worry, we never enforce that clause," assume they're lying.

DON'T assume your bonus will materialize. If it's not guaranteed in writing, it's just a nice idea.

DON'T ignore vague contract language. If something sounds sketchy, it probably is.

DON'T feel bad for asking questions. If they treat you like you're being difficult, imagine how they'll treat you once you actually work there.

At the end of the day, your offer letter isn't just an invitation to join a company; it's a contract that defines your financial future and career mobility. If you don't protect yourself now, you might regret it later. Read carefully, negotiate wisely, and most importantly, make sure you're signing up for what you actually want, not what they hope you won't notice.

CHAPTER ELEVEN

The First 90 Days: Set Yourself Up for Success

TL;DR

Your first 90 days at a new job are about setting yourself up for long-term success, not about proving you're the best hire of all time. First impressions stick. Overpromising is a trap. And if you're not paying attention to team dynamics, you're already behind. This chapter is your survival guide for those first three months without burning out, stepping on landmines, or accidentally becoming the office ghost. The difference between someone who just "gets through" their first 90 days and someone who nails it is not talent. It's strategy.

This chapter will walk you through the key moves that actually matter, from managing first impressions, building the right relationships, and setting realistic expectations to avoiding the classic traps that derail careers before they even start.

You 90-Day First Impression Window

You landed the job. Congratulations! Now, the real work begins, not just the actual work, but the delicate balancing act of figuring out how this place actually functions before you start making moves. Too many new hires show up on day one thinking they need to prove themselves immediately, volunteer for everything, push ideas before they understand the culture, and set expectations they'll regret later. Others take the opposite approach, laying low for too long and blending into the background so well that no one even remembers they were hired. Both strategies are bad bad bad.

Your goal in the first 90 days isn't to be a superstar. It's to become indispensable, strategically. That means learning before speaking, observing before acting, and making sure the right people see your value without setting yourself up for a lifetime of overwork.

Your first 90 days in a new job aren't about proving you're the smartest person in the room. They're about proving you belong in the room. First impressions stick, and once they're made, they're hard to change. People form subconscious judgments about your reliability, work ethic, and potential within weeks, influencing how they treat you, what opportunities come your way, and whether they trust you with important work.

These early impressions can be an asset or a liability. If you're seen as sharp, engaged, and thoughtful, that positive narrative follows you. Conversely, if you come in too aggressively—stepping on toes, overstepping boundaries, or trying to revolutionize workflows before understanding them—you'll spend months undoing that reputation. Instead of charging in with unsolicited ideas, spend those initial weeks watching, listening, and identifying what truly matters.

Many newcomers mistakenly believe they need to deliver immediate results. They take on excessive work, offer solutions before fully grasping problems, or attempt to lead without established credibility. The reality? These first three months are about setting the stage for long-term success, not sprinting to an imaginary finish line. Your objective isn't demonstrating how much you can do—it's understanding the landscape to recognize what's worth doing in the first place.

The people who succeed in the long term don't burn themselves out by proving they can work harder. They set themselves up to work smarter. Instead of trying to impress people with how much they can do, they do the following:

Observe before they act. Learn the company's culture, priorities, and decision-making process before jumping in.
Build relationships. Get to know the key players in the organization, not just their direct manager.
Manage expectations. Align their role, workload, and deliverables with the company's priorities.
Deliver steady, predictable value. Consistency builds trust far more than one-off bursts of effort.

A new hire who listens more than they talk, asks thoughtful questions, and delivers measured results is far more valuable than someone who rushes to contribute without fully understanding the landscape. If you spend your first 90 days learning how the company really works, you'll be in a much stronger position to drive meaningful impact down the road.

The bottom line is that your first three months set the tone for how people perceive you. They are not about hitting peak performance. I repeat: they are not about hitting peak performance. The first 90 days are about onboarding, integration, and credibility-building. The real work—the kind that gets you promoted, trusted, and brought into high-impact projects—happens after you've laid a strong foundation.

If you use your first 90 days wisely, you'll position yourself as someone who understands the bigger picture, navigates the company effectively, and adds value in a sustainable way. If you waste them trying to be an instant rockstar, you'll burn out, set expectations you can't maintain, or worse, you'll make a first impression you'll regret.

The Art of Being New

I have recently found myself thinking about all the unwritten corporate rules that exist. Throughout this book, I've talked about how job searching is kind of a game we all have to play, and I have bad news for you all: landing the job is just the beginning. Even the jobs you love at the companies you dream about are often full of unspoken rules and politics that can trip anybody up. Here's a big corporate truth: Once you have a bad reputation at work, it is nearly impossible to change it. And reputations are made *quickly*!

For most people, this means that once your boss and coworkers decide you're not a hard worker, or that you're a know-it-all, or that you rush and are a little sloppy, you'll probably never change their minds. This is why I focus so much on the first 90 days in this chapter. Sure, most of this stuff is good career advice no matter where you are, but the first three months at your new job have the potential to set you up for great success, or set the timer on how long you are going to last, and it is only partially related to any of the actual work that you do.

I have been fired from a job after six weeks, and I have hired people we had to let go in 30 days. I have seen people live off reputations they don't deserve, and I have been in the rooms where these private conversations about new hires happen. They don't teach this class at school, but I'm going to teach you some of the most important things to do in those first few months.

Integrate Without Overpromising

One of the biggest mistakes new hires make is coming in too hot, trying to impress everyone, only to end up overcommitted, misaligned with expectations, or on everyone's nerves. The smartest employees don't rush in guns blazing. They observe, adapt, and strategically integrate into the team before doing anything that could backfire.

A Real World Story

A guy I worked with, let's call him Jake, started a new job determined to prove himself. From day one, he was *everywhere.* He was volunteering for extra projects, pulling late nights, and saying yes to everything. Leadership noticed. His manager loved him. But here's the problem: Jake set his own trap. Three months in, he was drowning. What began as an impressive work ethic became the expectation. The second he tried to scale back, he wasn't seen as leveling out. He was seen as slipping.

One night, his boss sent him a "quick project" at 9 p.m., and Jake finally pushed back. His manager was confused: "You've always handled this before. Why can't you do this now?" Jake was exhausted. But to his boss, this wasn't a burnout problem. This was a performance drop. Within six months, Jake wasn't the rising star anymore. He was *barely hanging* on.

Mike's take: The big, important takeaway here is that however you start is how people expect you to continue. If you go above and beyond too early, you're setting the bar unsustainably high, and slowing down looks like failure. Jake set zero boundaries at work, which, to his boss, meant that he had none! Work hard, but pace yourself. Long-term success beats short-term heroics.

Your First-Few-Weeks Superpower: Observation

The urge to prove your worth right away is real. You got the job, and you want people to see why. But nothing screams *I have no idea what's going on* quite like jumping into conversations you don't fully understand. Your first job in a new role is not to fix everything. It's to figure out what actually needs fixing. Pay attention to how meetings run. Who actually makes decisions? What do you notice about the unspoken team culture? If you don't take the time to notice these things, you'll end up violating rules you didn't even know existed.

The Balance Between Confidence and Humility

Confidence doesn't mean talking the most or having all the answers; it means knowing when to ask the right questions and when to hold back. Nobody expects you to be an expert on day one, but they do expect you to be self-aware enough to learn before acting. Instead of barging in with suggestions, try framing things as questions: "I noticed the team does x. Why is that?" or "I saw [past project] worked really well. What made it successful?" These kinds of questions do two things. They show that you're paying attention, and they get people to engage with you.

A Real World Story: My Biggest New Job Error

You have probably figured out already that I'm very confident in what I do. I have had to learn the hard way that just because I was hired to make things better does not mean the expectation was that I come in on day one and start changing things. A frequent problem during my career has been showing up a bit too excited to work, full of ideas, and ready to break everything down and build it back up. This sounds great on paper, but nobody really loves being told how bad of a job they've been doing by the new guy who doesn't know that much yet. I have sat down with CEOs and just told them point-blank that what they are doing is not working and that we should do it my way instead. Do you want to guess how well those conversations went and how many of my day-one ideas were implemented quickly?

Mike's take: One of the best pieces of advice I can give a new hire is to spend more time listening and less time prescribing. You will gain a lot more buy-in when you prove you are making an effort to understand before just assuming you know better.

How to Ask Smart Questions Without Looking Unprepared

Asking questions is good. Asking obvious or lazy questions makes you look like you didn't do your homework. Where have I heard this before? Oh yeah, from me, earlier in this book. It was good advice on the job interview, and it's still good advice now that you have the job! Yes, there is definitely such a thing as asking too many questions, but the bigger offense is asking too many dumb questions. Note, two is probably too many.

Asking questions like, "I saw your recent launch of x. What was the biggest challenge the team faced rolling it out?" shows engagement without making you look like you weren't paying attention during onboarding. But asking something like "Where can I find this file?" after you were given login credentials to the company's shared drive and haven't bothered to look yet is wasting somebody's time.

Reading the Unspoken Rules: What They Won't Tell You in Orientation

Every workplace has *written* rules. These are the ones in the handbook. And every workplace also has *unwritten* rules. These are the ones you discover the hard way. Unwritten rules tend to dictate how meetings run. Are meetings formal? Does everyone speak or just the loudest person? Who holds the power? Is it the boss or their right-hand person? How fast do things move? Is this a "just ship it" culture or a "let's circle back" culture?

Pay close attention to communication styles. Does your team prefer Slack, email, or in-person chats? Understanding the primary channel where important decisions happen can save you from missing critical information. Notice the meeting culture too. Does everyone speak, or is it a leadership monologue? This tells you volumes about how ideas flow in your organization. Even expectations about responsiveness vary widely between workplaces. Are emails answered within an hour, or is 48 hours the norm? Learning these unspoken timelines helps you avoid appearing unresponsive or seeming too pushy.

The best way to learn these unwritten rules is to watch how people behave. Take note of how your team interacts, how decisions get made, and what behaviors are rewarded. It sounds a little sleazy, but pay attention to who leadership likes, which tends to be obvious. Sometimes they are the kinds of people with no problem puckering up and kissing a little backside, but sometimes they are also good workers who make meaningful contributions. What do the people the leadership likes do well? How do they do it? Why does leadership trust them? Figure out those answers and see if you can do those things too.

A common mistake? Jumping hierarchy. If you have a question, follow the chain of command. Don't email the CEO because you think it'll make you look proactive. Your manager will not appreciate being bypassed, and leadership will see it as a lack of understanding about how the organization functions.

The Expectations Trap: Underpromise, Overdeliver

Your first 90 days aren't just about learning the job. They're about setting the expectations for what people should expect from you forever. If you start out saying yes to everything, working late every night, and pulling off impossible deadlines, congratulations, you've just told everyone that's your normal speed. And guess what? They'll expect you to maintain that pace forever.

New hires often feel pressure to prove themselves immediately, leading them to overcommit. They say yes before fully understanding what's being asked, underestimate timelines, and equate more work with more value. The reality? This approach leaves them overwhelmed and drowning in self-imposed obligations. Remember: The workload you establish early becomes your baseline. Set that bar too high, and you'll be permanently stuck trying to clear it.

Without clarifying priorities, you risk chasing everything while missing what truly matters. Every workplace has unspoken priorities, things they value more than they say. If you don't uncover these hidden priorities, you'll waste energy on low-impact tasks while neglecting what actually moves the needle. Letting others define your expectations means you'll constantly be reacting rather than strategically driving your own success.

The advice to "underpromise, overdeliver" sounds simple but is often misapplied. Some set the bar embarrassingly low, while others create such generous deadlines that they appear unambitious. The real skill isn't underpromising; it's framing expectations in ways that highlight your intelligence, reliability, and strategic thinking.

Rather than blindly accepting deadlines, get comfortable asking clarifying questions: "Is this the top priority, or is there flexibility on timing?" "I can finish this by Friday. Does that timeline work?" "If I focus on this, I'll need to push x to next week. Which is more urgent?" These questions serve dual purposes: they demonstrate thoughtful prioritization while buying you time to deliver quality work.

Ultimately, underpromising isn't about doing less. It's about ensuring your contributions are high-impact rather than merely high-volume. New hires who master this approach quickly build a reputation as someone who manages their workload effectively, not just someone churning out work without strategic consideration.

A Real World Success Story

I once had a new hire ask the best question I've ever heard on his first day. Instead of trying to impress everyone immediately, he pulled his manager aside and asked, "What's one thing I should focus on in my first 90 days that will make your life easier?" It was a brilliant move. First, it reframed the conversation. He wasn't just thinking about his success. He was thinking about how to add value to the team. Second, his manager gave him gold: clear priorities, insight into what actually mattered, and an immediate inside track on how to make an impact. A year later? That hire was on a leadership track.

Mike's take: Instead of trying to prove yourself with grand gestures, ask smart, targeted questions. The people who listen before they act end up ahead of the ones who rush to make noise.

The first few months are a marathon, not a sprint. Establish credibility and set the standard of how you work and what it will be like to work with you. Some new hires try to outwork everyone immediately, setting a bar they won't be able to sustain and ruffling the feathers of key players on the team. Others hold back too much and miss their chance to prove themselves. The goal is steady, reliable effort that builds momentum over time. Be predictably good, not sporadically great.

Being new is an opportunity to be the person you want to be at this job. At the same time, it is also a potential trap that can have you back on the job market and re-reading the first few chapters of this book sooner than you'd hoped! You have a window where people expect you to ask questions, learn fast, and integrate into the team. If you use that time wisely, you set the stage for long-term success. But if you waste it trying too hard or failing to read the room, you'll spend months trying to fix the impression you made in your first few weeks, and you'll probably never really correct that first impression. So slow down. Listen more than you talk. And remember that nobody expects you to be a superstar on day one. All they want is for you not to make them regret hiring you.

SIDEBAR

Awwww. Is this our last sidebar? I'm going to miss our little chats about how frustrating some of this stuff is. Look, I'll say it. So much of this stuff is icky. It doesn't feel good to write. It doesn't feel good to talk about. It doesn't feel good to do. But as I've said over and over again, it is what it is! I would love a world where office politics don't exist, but they do. Not only that, but they can wreak havoc in your daily life and your career. You will hear a lot of people tell you never to trust anyone at work and that you aren't there to make friends, but I don't believe that. I think relationships at work are incredibly important, and yes, one day someone may hurt you, but also the opposite could happen too! So, when I dive into this next part of the book, please don't judge me as some kind of corporate "pick me!" Understand that we all need to navigate these things, but very few people talk about them openly. I'm going to. My hope is that you'll read this book, benefit from it, and then pass it along to someone else who needs it. That means not messing this all up and needing the whole book again too quickly! Okay? Great, let's get out there and talk about work relationships.

Building the Right Relationships

Unfortunately, in any job, success isn't just about doing good work. Another one of those unwritten rules nobody teaches is that visibility is just as important as performance in many workplaces. The first 90 days of your job aren't just about learning your role. They're about identifying who shapes how the work gets done and making sure the right people notice the right things.

The Hidden Hierarchy: Who Makes the Decisions?

very company operates with two distinct layers of authority that you must understand to navigate successfully. While the org. chart shows who technically possesses decision-making power, the influence network reveals who actually gets things done. Focusing solely on job titles means missing the people who truly control priorities, budgets, and workflow. Though leadership ultimately signs off on decisions, the people shaping those decisions often work behind the scenes. These influential figures include department gatekeepers who control access to leadership, the trusted "right hand" whom leaders confide in and always consult for opinions, and the "informal leaders" – those tenured employees everyone turns to for real advice. Recognizing this dual power structure is essential for effectively navigating workplace dynamics.

Who You Need to Build Relationships With and Who to Avoid

Some people in your company will help you move forward, while others will inevitably drag you into office drama. The first 90 days present a crucial opportunity to align yourself with the right people and steer clear of potential bad influences. Prioritize building relationships with your boss (obviously), your immediate team members, who shape your day-to-day reality, cross-functional partners outside your team, who impact your work, and key decision-makers whose opinions genuinely sway leadership.

At the same time, be vigilant about those you should approach with caution: the chronic complainer who loves to vent but rarely takes action, the fake mentor who initially seems helpful but is actually gathering intelligence, and the office politician who constantly works angles for personal gain.

Aligning with the right people builds your visibility and credibility, while getting too close to the wrong people can entangle you in workplace politics before you even realize what's happening. I cannot stress enough how much damage association with chronic complainers can do to your reputation and career prospects. These individuals may not realize it, but everyone, including leadership, knows exactly who they are. Their constant complaining and non-constructive approach to issues gets noticed and remembered. While venting occasionally might feel necessary, you absolutely don't want to become known as this person, nor do you want to be the sympathetic ear they seek when looking to drag someone else into their negativity.

Make Casual but Strategic Conversation

Some of the most important career moves happen outside of formal meetings in hallway chats, Slack conversations, and post-meeting debriefs. If you only speak when spoken to, you're essentially making yourself invisible to the people who matter. The real skill lies in simply engaging naturally without forcing connections. To build strong, low-pressure professional relationships, focus on making thoughtful observations rather than resorting to meaningless small talk, for instance, comment on someone's project strategy breakdown and ask about their approach. Similarly, request insights rather than favors, perhaps by acknowledging a colleague's tenure and asking what new hires typically overlook. Finally, offer genuine assistance where appropriate. Express your willingness to lend a hand on projects without overcommitting. These seemingly casual interactions create the foundation for strategic relationships that can significantly impact your professional growth and visibility within the organization.

Office Politics: Play Smart and Don't Get Played

Workplace politics exist whether you like them or not. You don't have to play dirty, but you do need to be aware of the underlying dynamics that shape your work environment. As you settle in, pay close attention to the order of operations regarding information flow. Notice who consistently learns about developments first (typically the "right-hand" people) and who finds out last. This pattern rarely changes. Information almost always passes through the same chain of custody by design, not by accident. While going full *Game of Thrones* and eliminating everyone above you isn't the goal, building trust with those high up the information chain is invariably beneficial.

It is just as important to observe how disagreement with leadership unfolds. Most companies feature three broad types: those who simply nod along with whatever leadership proposes, those who speak up and are genuinely heard, and those who voice opinions only to be consistently ignored. Recognizing where different colleagues fall—and understanding your own position in this spectrum—provides crucial insight into the company's real power structure. Ignoring these dynamics risks marginalization, while overengagement makes you part of the drama. Your wisest initial approach? Maintain neutrality, carefully observe the real influencers, and gradually align yourself with those focused on delivering results rather than gossiping.

The bottom line is that your first 90 days are a relationship-building game as much as they are a performance game. You can be great at your job, but if the right people don't see your value, it won't matter. If you focus only on tasks and ignore the human dynamics, you'll miss half the picture. The people who understand the power structure early, engage strategically, and avoid unnecessary politics set themselves up for long-term success. Everyone else? They just do the work and wonder why they're always left out of the bigger conversations.

How to Communicate Effectively At Work

So far I have given a lot of advice about setting boundaries, building relationships with the right people, and pushing back at the right time, but what I haven't done is talk about how. Just like I said about negotiation earlier, so much of this is about the how, not the if! Being able to deliver tough or awkward information is a huge trait of successful employees.

Pushing back isn't about being uncooperative. It's about framing the conversation to set yourself up for long-term success. Too many new hires think they have to say yes to everything to be seen as a team player. The truth is that saying yes to everything makes you look inexperienced and sets you up for failure. People who know their worth and their capacity don't just accept every task thrown at them. Don't just say no if you need to push back on a request. Instead, reframe the conversation: "I'd love to take that on. What should I deprioritize to fit it in?" "That's a great idea, and I want to do it well. Can we extend the deadline?" "I'm happy to own this. What resources and support would be available?" This keeps you from looking like someone just rejecting work, while ensuring you don't overcommit to something you can't deliver on. If you set the expectation early that you prioritize strategically, you'll be seen as a smart operator, not just a task robot.

Not every issue needs to be raised the second you notice it. You can take a beat. The smartest employees know when to speak up and when to hold off. Raising concerns too early, before you have the full picture, can make you seem reactionary rather than thoughtful. But waiting too long to address something critical can make you look checked out or ineffective. Knowing when to speak up is about reading the room, the timing, and the impact.

It is a good idea to speak up when deadlines, responsibilities, or expectations aren't clear, when a small problem is about to snowball into a major issue, and when you aren't going to be able to meet a demand and need to reprioritize. On the other hand, you should hold off when you're brand new and don't have full context yet, when the issue is minor and wouldn't significantly change anything, when something new is introduced and you assume you won't like it, or when you're frustrated but don't have a solution to offer.

A Real World Success Story

I used to work with someone who had a problem with nearly any suggestion or new idea. Anytime something was implemented, no matter how minor, they would always ask why and ask a bunch of questions that didn't really need to be answered. They would see what holes they could poke in the new idea before just letting it play out. In their mind, they were seeking clarity, but to most people, they were just derailing brainstorming sessions or were afraid of change. This became that coworker's reputation despite their good work, and they found themselves at the bottom of those information chains I mentioned earlier because everyone knew how they would respond anyway.

> **Mike's take:** I know this person meant well, and you probably know people like this. Heck, maybe you are this guy. But what they saw as seeking clarity was really just constant negativity. If there is a real problem with an idea, raise it, but if you're just pointing out how it may not be pulled off perfectly, you should probably save that until things play out a little bit. Just because you wouldn't do it this way doesn't mean that it's bad or not worth trying.

The way you communicate with your peers and leaders has a huge effect on your work experience. Like everything in this chapter, it's all about balance. You don't want to be seen as passive and nonchalant, but it's just as important not to be seen as someone who has a problem with everything and can never just go with it. Your tone and word choice are important, and being able to have tough conversations without sounding combative is a skill you must cultivate.

What I Wish I'd Known Sooner

A big theme of this chapter is that nobody actually teaches you how to succeed in corporate America. They give you tired advice like "just network," or "be the first one in," but they don't *really* talk about what so many workplaces are like. I spent so much of the early part of my career being a loyal dedicated employee because I was taught that's what would get me ahead, but it didn't. But I also see too many people who think they can just coast off vibes and make it to the top. Spoiler: you can't! Getting ahead in the corporate world is a combination of so many factors beyond just good work or having a rich relative. Okay, maybe having a rich relative can help, but it's not the only way. Let's talk about some of the real lessons I've learned along the way that focus less on clickbait ideas like "be the personality hire" and more on what people really want to see at work.

Respect + Trust > Being the Office Favorite

In your first 90 days, you'll feel a totally natural urge to make people like you. It's understandable. You want to fit in, be accepted, and not rock the boat too much. But you're playing the wrong game if you prioritize being liked over being respected. Respect gets you opportunities. Likeability is a bonus.

The people who get ahead in their careers aren't necessarily the most fun to be around, but they are the people trusted to get things done. That doesn't mean you have to be cold or transactional, but it does mean that your goal should be to establish yourself as competent and reliable before worrying about whether you're the office favorite. Respect means people trust your work, seek your input, and listen when you speak. And being that person usually comes with being well-liked. Nobody ever says, "That person is too reliable and competent. Let's not talk to them!"

No, Your Work Won't Speak for Itself

A lot of smart, hardworking professionals assume that if they do great work, they'll be noticed and rewarded. That's some Disney movie stuff, because sadly, out here in the real world, it doesn't work that way. In reality, companies are full of people doing good work, and the people who get ahead are the ones who make sure their contributions are visible.

Self-advocacy isn't about bragging. It's about making sure people know the impact of what you're doing. If you quietly do great work and assume someone will notice, you'll be disappointed waiting for that pat on the back. You need to share your wins and toot your own horn. Nobody is going to toot it for you.

How do you share your wins? Keep leadership updated on your work. Send a quick recap email after big projects. Speak up in meetings when your work is relevant. Frame your updates in terms of impact: "This project streamlined x-process, saving the team y hours per week." That way, you're not just reporting what you did. You're showing *why it matters.*

Manage Up: Make Your Boss's Life Easier Without Being a Doormat

A lot of people misunderstand what it means to "manage up." They think it means being extra agreeable, taking on more work, or anticipating every possible request. In reality, managing up is about understanding your boss's priorities, making their job easier, and ensuring you're aligned with what they actually care about.

A great employee doesn't just do their job well. They also make their manager look good. That means keeping them informed without overloading them, solving problems before they become fires, and figuring out leadership's priorities so you can align your efforts accordingly.

Want to get on your boss's good side? Make their life easier in ways that actually help. Send proactive updates before they have to ask. Solve issues at your level before they escalate. And most importantly, understand what they need to look good to their boss. If you can help them with that, you become indispensable.

Work Hard *and* Play the Game

Hard work alone won't get you ahead. Understanding how success actually works in your company will. Too many people assume that grinding away at their desk is the path to recognition, but the reality is that promotions, raises, and opportunities go to those who align themselves with leadership priorities, build visibility, and connect their work to big-picture goals.

If you want to move up, you need to learn what your boss's boss cares about because that's what dictates strategy. You need to understand the company's long-term goals because aligning with them makes you look indispensable. And you need to make sure your work doesn't exist in a vacuum. If leadership doesn't see it, it might as well not exist.

The best employees don't just execute tasks; they position themselves as people who drive outcomes. If you can demonstrate that your work directly impacts things that matter to leadership, you'll be ahead of 90% of your peers.

Your first 90 days aren't just about learning how to do your job. They're about learning how to position yourself for long-term success. That means:

Prioritize being respected over being liked. Friendships are great, but credibility gets you promoted.
Make sure your work is visible. If no one knows what you're doing, it doesn't matter how great your work is.
Manage up effectively. Align with your boss's priorities. Keep them informed, and solve problems before they escalate.
Understand the bigger picture. The people who move up aren't just hard workers. They're the ones who connect their work to leadership's goals.

Work smart, not just hard. Your career isn't just about what you do; it's about how you position yourself, who sees your contributions, and whether you're playing the long game. If you get this right early on, you won't just do well in your first 90 days, you'll set yourself up for success in the long term.

Common New-Hire Pitfalls to Avoid

Unfortunately, I've seen a lot of quick turnover in my career. Sometimes, it is because of managers who don't know what they want, or because someone was just not as good as we hoped, but often, it's just a matter of not really understanding behaviors that don't work well in the workplace. Skills like self-reliance and self-advocacy are so important. What happens when you aren't self-reliant and don't advocate for yourself?

Why You Need to Be Self-Sufficient Early

Some new hires treat their managers like a personal GPS, constantly checking in, waiting for step-by-step directions, and never making a move without explicit approval. This approach makes you appear passive, high-maintenance, and lacking resourcefulness. Your manager doesn't want to babysit you. They want someone who can think independently. The key difference between a high-performing new hire and one who struggles is initiative. You don't need all the answers, but you should be able to figure things out without using your manager as a human instruction manual. Instead of asking "What should I do next?" try "I've developed this plan. Does it align with our priorities?" This demonstrates initiative rather than permission seeking. Or you might say, "I see two potential approaches to this. Do you have a preference, or should I proceed with my recommendation?" This presents options instead of problems. Another effective approach is "After researching previous projects, I noticed x. Should I follow that precedent, or would you prefer a different direction?" This shows you've done your homework before seeking guidance.

Remember, your manager hired you to solve problems, not create more work for them. By approaching your role with autonomy and thoughtfulness, you'll build trust faster and position yourself as a valuable team member rather than just another direct report. This self-sufficient mindset not only makes your manager's life easier but also accelerates your own professional growth and advancement opportunities.

Not Documenting Early Wins: Track Your Own Progress

The first 90 days aren't just about learning, they're about proving you belong. If you don't track your contributions, no one else will. And when it's time to talk about promotions, raises, or future opportunities, you'll be competing against people who kept receipts. Your early wins are proof of your value. If you don't document them, you're relying on other people to notice and remember. And spoiler alert: they won't. There are several ways to track your wins without appearing self-absorbed. Keep a private running list of completed projects, improvements, or contributions. Save positive feedback from coworkers and managers, including Slack messages, emails, and performance notes. Summarize your impact in quantifiable terms. "Reducing processing time by 30%" sounds much more impressive than "Helped out with some reports." Bring up your accomplishments strategically. When your manager asks how things are going, mention something concrete: "I implemented x last month, and it's already saved the team 473 hours."

Advancing in your career depends on your ability to advocate for yourself with the receipts. You can't just hope someone notices your hard work. By systematically documenting your contributions, you're building a compelling narrative about your value that will serve you throughout your career. This isn't bragging. It's about taking ownership of your professional story and ensuring your efforts translate into opportunities.

Preparing for Your First Performance Review... and Beyond

Your first formal performance review might not be scheduled for months, but don't let that fool you. It's already happening. The moment you start a new job, people are evaluating you, and not just your boss, but your coworkers, cross-functional partners, and anyone else who has a say in how you're evaluated. If you wait until your actual review to start thinking about how you're doing, you've already lost the game.

Smart employees don't leave their success up to chance; they track their impact from day one. Keep a running list of what you've worked on, what you've improved, and what results you've driven. If you've streamlined a process, fixed a broken workflow, or knocked a project out of the park, write it down! When review time comes, you don't want to rely on fuzzy feelings of *I think I did well.*

Here's a pro move: Ask for feedback before you need it. A casual check-in with your manager at the one- or two-month mark can reveal whether you're on the right track or if you need to make adjustments before it's too late. When I'm in charge, I bake these into your first month or two by default, but not everyone will. After 30 days, don't be scared to send your boss a quick note , something like, "Hey, I'd love to touch base about my first month, talk through some things I think are going well, and see what kind of feedback you may have for me." If you get critical feedback early, you can fix it before it shows up in your first official performance review. If you get positive feedback, you can double down on what's working. Either way, you're taking control instead of just passively hoping for the best.

End Your First 90 Days with Momentum

There's a weird phenomenon that happens after onboarding. Some employees slow down. The big rush of learning, meeting people, and figuring things out settles, and they slip into maintenance mode. That's fine if all you want is to keep your job. But if you want to actually grow in your career, your first 90 days aren't the finish line. They're the launchpad.

How do you keep momentum going after onboarding? First, don't stop asking questions. Just because you're no longer the "new hire" doesn't mean you should suddenly pretend you know everything. Keep learning, seeking context, and making sure you understand the bigger picture of your work.

Second, set personal goals beyond your official job description. What do you want to be known for on this team? What skills do you want to build? What areas of the business do you want to learn more about? If you wait for someone else to define your growth, you're just reacting. If you set your own targets, you're directing where you want to go.

And finally, don't let relationships fade. All those people you connected with in the first 90 days? Follow up with them. Keep those relationships active. Check in with your boss before you need something.

Your first 90 days set the stage for the rest of your career at this company. If you treat onboarding like a one-time event instead of the foundation for what's next, you're already falling behind. Track your wins, start thinking about your growth early, and don't let momentum slip just because you're no longer technically a new hire.

Mike's Snarky Do's and Don'ts of Job Searching

DO slow down before making changes. Nobody wants to hear your "big ideas" before you even know what's broken.

DO read the room. Pay attention to who holds real power. Hint: It's not always the person with the title.

DO manage expectations early. If you start at 110%, that's your new baseline forever.

DO track your wins. If you don't document them, they don't exist.

DO make yourself visible, but don't be obnoxious. Speak up in meetings when you have something to add, but don't force yourself into every conversation.

DON'T try to fix things before you understand them. The process you're about to "optimize" might be broken for a reason.

DON'T attach yourself to the office complainer. Nothing tanks your reputation faster than aligning with the wrong people.

DON'T be too reliant on your boss. If you need their approval for every tiny decision, you're a liability, not an asset.

DON'T assume your work will speak for itself. If no one knows what you've done, you didn't actually do it.

DON'T disappear after onboarding. The first 90 days aren' the finish line. They're just the start.

At the end of the day, your first 90 days determine your trajectory. You can either be the person who gets noticed for all the right reasons or the one who quietly blends in until people forget you exist. Play this game right, and you won't just survive. You'll set yourself up to thrive.

Epilogue: You're Gonna Need This Again. That's Not a Threat. It's Just Capitalism.

If you're here, reading the final pages, first of all, *congrats.* You stuck it out longer than most hiring managers reviewing resumes. You've officially demonstrated more commitment than half of the companies ghosting candidates right now.

Thank you for giving yourself the space to learn this messy, demoralizing, oddly strategic, wildly emotional thing we call the job search. Because now you get it: This isn't just a moment. It's a skill set. And you've got it now.

Will the job market magically become fair and efficient because you've read this? No. Will companies stop asking for 12 years of experience in software invented last quarter? Also no. But you'll stop taking it personally. You'll stop spinning every rejection into a referendum on your entire existence. And when the process inevitably sucks, you'll know how to move through it instead of getting flattened by it.

You now have a system. You've got frameworks, tools, stories, and just enough sarcastic commentary lodged in your brain to keep you going when someone says, "We're going in a different direction" after a seven-round interview marathon and a presentation you had to make in Canva. And when that happens, you won't crumble. You'll sigh. You'll roll your eyes. You'll text a friend, "lol I hate this," close your laptop for an hour, and then get back to work. Not because you're a machine, but because now you *actually know what you're doing.*

Let's be real: You're going to job search again. Even if this time ends with the perfect role at the perfect company with coworkers who pronounce your name correctly and don't use "circle back" unironically, something will eventually change. That's not a sign that you failed. It's a sign that you're still growing.

So don't shelf this book like a souvenir from your time in the trenches. Keep it around. Keep it dog-eared, highlighted, and full of passive-aggressive notes in the margins. Come back to it when you're curious, when you're stuck, when you're spiraling, or when you need a reminder that no, you're not crazy. This whole system is.

And maybe, when you're on the other side, you'll help someone else who's in the middle of it. Share what you've learned.

Send them this book. Be the person who says, "Yeah, it's a mess. But you can learn to navigate it. I did."

At the end of the day, this isn't just about getting a job. It's about knowing your worth, owning your story, and showing up like someone who understands that being judged is part of the deal.

So go on. Land the job. Crush the interview. Negotiate the hell out of your offer. And when you do? I'll be in the background, or more likely the TikTok comments arguing with people too scared to use a real photo or a real name who refuse to listen to me, cheering you on!

And if it all falls apart later? Cool. You've learned how to build the fire escape, so get building again!

Acknowledgments

This feels like a lot of pressure. I asked ChatGPT for help, and it said to keep this general and not name anyone specifically so that I don't leave anyone out. Fuck that! I'm naming names, and if you got left out, I'll just say the editors cut it for space. And if I include you and you don't mention it to me, I'm leaving you out of the next edition for not reading this part.

First and foremost, I want to thank my readers and social media followers—whether you randomly found me or were one of those first people spiraling with me—you are the reason I do this. Your stories, struggles, and triumphs have kept me creating content. You found me and trusted me, and I'll never understand why. But thank you for changing my life!

I want to thank Kerry, who got laid off 15 minutes before me, texted me to let me know, and said my meeting was probably just to tell me about her being laid off. You found a new job in like 45 minutes and have held it down as I've gone through twelve career pivots. That speaks to how good at this job you are. You were the only person in this entire industry who was there for me when I didn't know anyone. You used to tell me I'd be a great influencer before I even had a TikTok account, and then you became my first TikTok follower. You watched the view count tick up on my first-ever viral video, and the second it hit one million views, you texted me. I'm very sure I would not have done any of this without you pushing me. You are a true friend, even if I stopped texting you daily once I had my shit together!

My thanks also go out to the job seekers who became true friends. Sam, you made one of the first snarky comments I ever got on my TikTok. If it happened today, I'd probably block you, but I really wanted everyone to like me back then. I won you over, and then you coached me through my own anxiety spirals. Khrys, you will forever be the protagonist of an anecdote I tell about the power of real networks. (Your story is in this book with a fake name.) Kat, you helped me with industry knowledge I never had. The rest of you are thanked in the first part, so don't be mad that I left you out.

I am deeply grateful for my mentors, colleagues, and peers

along the way. Thank you for noticing me, accepting me, encouraging me, and becoming my friends. I have to mention Scott Moore, who convinced me I'd make a good recruiter a very long time ago when all I wanted was some fucking resume help. Dan and Farah, my CPP besties, did so much to prop me up in front of their audiences at the beginning. Joel, you called me on a Friday evening after I DMed you my number and told me I was on the verge of something big and to just keep going. The next day, I had my first viral video. And the rest is history. I don't know if you caused it, but I think you did. Amy|Hack Your HR, you started about the same time as me and have been 100,000x more successful, but you'd never know it from talking to you. Your constant support, kind words, and validation mean a lot. But none of it will ever mean as much as you canceling a meeting (with someone else) the day I got fired and hopping on a call with me just to see how I was. Kayte—my work BFF who helped edit the first pitch I ever made to speak at a conference, and also just always actually cared about me—we had the perfect mix of Slack convos and simultaneous not-for-Slack text convos! Lia Z., you were the first person ever to offer me money to make a TikTok. I only had about 5K followers at the time, and I did not understand. You said you saw something in me. I will always remember that after I posted that video, you commented, "A star is born." I still don't see it, but I'm so grateful that you did! Leah, becoming your friend has been an honor, working with you for seven minutes was fun too! And Morgan, deadass thank you for the drip assist. I was giving dad vibes, now giving main character, no cap.

This project would not have been possible without the incredible team at Purple Acorn and Gently Ventures who helped me put this book together. Evan, you just casually mentioned this option in passing and had no idea that a week later, I'd be on board. Dave and Nate, I'll miss our Thursday meetings, your excitement to share the week's developments, followed by the inevitable letdown of my being so unimpressed by everything. Yedida, editing me has to be a giant pain in the ass. You're getting so close to even being able to sound like me. Maybe next time.

I have already dedicated this book to my family, but hey, I'll mention you again because my wife Karen keeps asking how many times she will be mentioned in the book. Consider yourselves both thanked and dedicated to!

And finally, because I'm me, I must acknowledge the trolls, both online and in real life. I'm a petty guy, and some of you just have this way of making me want to prove you so fucking wrong. C, I was so excited to learn from you and emulate how respected you are in the industry. I remember thinking you'd teach me how to get on podcasts or noticed—LOL! My six weeks working on your team and how it ended is my villain origin story, so I should thank you because this book wouldn't have happened without that experience. To the people who wrote the following TikTok comments: "Six months and this guy will become irrelevant," "You are on the express lane to cancer," and "You have nothing of value to offer." I saved them, and I read them every time I wanted to stop and thought about this moment. Hey, I even marked on my calendar when the six-month mark had passed. I'm probably going to DM the three of you with a link to the preorder and ask what you've been up to since you wrote those comments.

Made in the USA
Las Vegas, NV
08 September 2025

25ce3cfd-6016-4e05-a28d-a44b321282f0R01